CONSIDER THESE THINGS WITH ME

Trying to Find the Right Way When
There Seems to be no Right Way

James Perry

CONSIDER THESE THINGS WITH ME

Copyright © 2010 by James Perry

All rights reserved. No part of this book may be reproduced or transmitted in any form or by any means without written permission of the author.

ISBN 9780984570867

A DEDICATION

I have been privileged to have known several people who have left an impression upon my life and the list would include many.

However, the one person who stands out above all others in my life is my precious wife, Peggy Ann Fry Perry. She qualifies as a rare jewel. She is a godly woman who reads and knows God's Word; is faithful in Prayer; and is a great encouragement to me as we have pursued different types of education and ministry situations for almost fifty-five years. We have been involved in Pastoral Ministry for more than forty-six years of our time together. God has used her to touch the lives of others as well and she has served faithfully and well.

She is my best friend and the most important person who serves as my ongoing inspiration. We have lived in all different kinds of places that were challenging - but my Precious Peggy never complained. She cheerfully pitched-in and can always be counted upon to try and make a difference – and – to do it with joy.

This is not just a Dedication statement but also a Tribute to one has meant more to me than anyone else could or will.

Foreword

The Word of God has always been a significant part of my life – from a Grandmother who both knew it and quoted it daily – to Sunday School Teachers who assigned verses and passages to memorize.

These pages contain a sense of the times in which we live and Biblical Principles that can enable us to find and follow the correct path for our lives. They represent articles and Blogs I have written that have been edited and taken out of the context that originally brought them to mind. Three passages of Scripture that occur to me often, as I reflect and as I write are - - -

Proverbs 14:12 (NLT) There is a path before each person that seems right, but it ends in death.

Proverbs 3:5-6 (NKJV) Trust in the Lord with all your heart, And lean not on your own understanding; In all your ways acknowledge Him, And He shall direct your paths.

Jeremiah 29:11-13 (NIV) For I know the plans I have for you, declares the Lord, plans to prosper you and not to harm you, plans to give you hope and a future. Then you will call upon me and come and pray to me, and I will listen to you. You will seek me and find me when you seek me with all your heart.

My hope is that you will want to fit your life into His Plans for you.

Table of Contents

The Old Grey Mare 1
When Humpty Dumpty Begins to Fall 9
Hopeless, Helpless, and Homeless 17
Wanted - Effective Leaders 23
Virtuous Vacillations 31
Life, Liberty and the Pursuit of. 39
Insulting More Than Intelligence 45
A Man's Word is His Bond (Or Is It?) 51
Applauding a Train Wreck 59
Phlegmatic Philosophy 65
Hyphenated-Fixation 71
What is Truth? - What is Fiction? 77
Should Topsy-Turvy Be Cloned? 85
The Pig's Last Oink and Squeal 95
Apple-Carts and Turnovers 101
Expectations Versus Abiliities 107
Dispossessing God 113
Unimaginable and Unprecedented 119
Tulipomania and Hoopla 125
Matters of the Heart 131
Gumption and Unction 137

Myrmidons	145
Forms of Filicide	149
Enfilading	153
Foundational Dysfunction?	159
Flummoxed	165
Revolting Development	171
Concluding Thoughts	177

The Old Grey Mare

The folk song expresses that – "The Old Grey Mare, Ain't what she used to be – Many long years ago!" The picture is of a horse – head drooped, sway backed, gait unsteady – the old grey mare…! What should be done to/for The Old Grey Mare? There seems to be only two choices – let her roam in the pasture freely, or have her put down (sent to a glue factory for processing). The process at the Glue Factory that occurs is: "(the) …prolonged boiling of animal connective tissue. These protein colloid glues are formed through hydrolysis of the collagen from skins, bones, tendons, and other tissues, similar to gelatin. These proteins form a molecular bond with the glued object. Stereotypically, the animal in question is a horse, and horses that are put down are often said to have been sent to the glue factory." The product was popular for woodworking prior to synthetic glues being developed. It could be argued that even in death the remains of The Old Grey Mare were useful.

Applying "The Old Grey Mare" to human life and plans for The Aging population: In October 2009, Business Specialties Investment had an item entitled: "The Graying of America: Age and Opportunity." They wrote: "America is getting older. According to current-year estimates from Nielsen Claritas, the 55-and-over crowd now represents 74 million people, or 24 percent of the total U.S. population. Considering the sheer size of this group and the wealth they control, life in an aging world must be seriously considered. Unlike our culture's obsession with the youth over the past 50 years, our future will be based on the interests of older people. According to the U.S. Census, 2037 will be our oldest year, with nearly 30 percent of households being headed by a person over 65. Forty-eight percent will be single-person households…What opportunities does an aging population offer? The market's clear demand for retirement housing is the primary beneficiary. Why? Economic cycles have little or no effect on the natural aging process and the healthcare needs they represent. Demand for hospitals and conveniently located medical facilities will continue to increase. The demand for affordable seniors housing, particularly in ethnic communities currently under-served, is already a reality. Since the facts support that The Graying of America is a dramatic demographic mega-trend shaping our landscape, serious investors can't afford not to consider the impact seniors will have on future real estate needs. Working with changing demographic trends, rather than against them, is the best way to reduce investment risk--and likely enhance returns…" One is forced to muse – is this the general sentiment of the American government toward the aging in the nation? Or – have the aged become too much of a liability for a nation whose bent is for redistribution of wealth and benefits, etc.?

      In a broader view, is there a distinction that can be made in The Aging Process between knowledge and wisdom? Is senility, dementia, Alzheimer's, and general forgetfulness inevitable? Is the older person to be relegated to a Nursing Home (pasture) or a worse fate – "Put Down" (euthanasia)? Is there a possibility that in the tendencies of youth there is a loss in perspective of the value of wisdom attained over the years versus the knowledge that is intellectually acquired? In Leviticus 19:32, the Lord says: "You shall stand up before the gray head and honor the face of an old man, and you shall fear your God: I am the Lord." Another translation (NLT) states: "Show your fear of God by standing up in the presence of elderly people and showing respect for the aged. I am the Lord." Solomon wrote in Proverbs 23:22, "Listen to your father who gave you life, and do not despise your mother when she is old." In Jeremiah's lament – Lamentations 5:11-17 – because of rebellion against the Lord, and embracing of sin, we read: "Our enemies rape the women and young girls…Our princes are being hanged by their thumbs, and THE OLD MEN ARE TREATED WITH CONTEMPT. The young men are led away to work at millstones, and the children stagger under heavy loads of wood. THE OLD MEN NO LONGER SIT IN THE CITY GATES (the place of wisdom); the young men no longer dance and sing. The joy of our hearts has ended; our dancing has turned to mourning. The garlands have fallen from our heads. Disaster has fallen upon us because we have sinned. Our hearts are sick and weary, and our eyes grow dim with tears." Our nation may be well down a similar road – is it too late for it to reverse its course?

Considerable attention is given to the subject of aging - senility, dementia, Alzheimer's, general forgetfulness – plus the additional focus on Medicare Costs, Social Security and general health issues. In terms of Social Security and Medicare Costs, few are willing to address the fact that the monies paid into Social Security during one's younger and productive years were not invested or saved for payment of benefits in one's latter years – but were spent on other budget expenditures. The broad point is: Are those in the aging process no longer able to be productive and useful?

An interesting article appeared January 3rd, 2010 by Barbara Strauch (Adult Learning - Neuroscience) entitled: "How To Train The Aging Brain." She speaks of reading many fine tomes, but observes: "I love reading history, and the shelves in my living room are lined with fat, fact-filled books…The problem is, as much as I've enjoyed these books, I don't really remember reading any of them. Certainly I know the main points. But didn't I, after underlining all those interesting parts, retain anything else? It's maddening and, sorry to say, not all that unusual for a brain at middle age: I don't just forget whole books, but movies I just saw, breakfasts I just ate, and the names, oh, the names are awful. Who are you? Brains in middle age, which, with increased life spans, now stretches from the 40s to late 60s, also get more easily distracted. Start boiling water for pasta, go answer the doorbell and — whoosh — all thoughts of boiling water disappear. Indeed, aging brains, even in the middle years, fall into what's called the default mode, during which the mind wanders off and begin daydreaming. Given all this, the question arises, can an old brain learn, and then remember what it learns? As it happens, yes. While it's tempting to focus on the flaws in older brains, that inducement overlooks how capable they've become. Over the past several years, scientists have looked deeper into how brains age and confirmed that they continue to develop through and beyond middle age. Many long-held views, including the one that 40 percent of brain cells are lost, have been overturned. What is stuffed into your head may not have vanished but has simply been squirreled away in the folds of your neurons… Recently, researchers have found even more positive news. The brain, as it traverses middle age, gets better at recognizing the central idea, the big picture. If kept in good shape, the brain can continue to build pathways that help its owner recognize patterns and, as a consequence, see significance and even solutions much faster than a young person can…Educators say that, for adults, one way to nudge neurons in the right direction is to challenge the very assumptions they have worked so hard to accumulate while young. With a brain already full of well-connected pathways, adult learners should 'jiggle their synapses a bit' by confronting thoughts that are contrary to their own…"

    Many err by not having appreciation for the older and aging person. So many experiences and knowledge that could be shared are ignored and avoided. The wisdom that could be of benefit is not embraced. An illustration of this is in I Kings 12:1-11, "Rehoboam went to Shechem, for all Israel had come…to make him king…and all…Israel came and said to Rehoboam: Your father made our yoke heavy. Now therefore lighten the hard service of your father and his heavy yoke on us, and we will serve you. He said to them, Go away for three days, then come again to me…King Rehoboam took counsel with the old men, who had stood before Solomon his father while he was yet alive, saying, How do you advise me to answer this people? They said to him, If you will be a servant to this people today and serve them, and speak good words to them when you answer them, then they will be your servants forever. But he abandoned the counsel that the old men gave him and took counsel with the young men who had grown up with him and stood before him…What do you advise that we answer this people…And the young men…said to him, Thus shall you speak to this people who said to you, Your father made our yoke heavy… My little finger is thicker than my father's thighs. And now, whereas my father laid on you a heavy yoke, I will add to your yoke. My father disciplined you with whips, but I will discipline you with scorpions." A clear example of the avoidance of wisdom; A missed opportunity; A lost moment to make a difference; Ignoring the Older Generation and embracing the Folly of Youth! It still occurs – but it doesn't have to continue!

The process of aging can have many peaks and valleys – the death of loved ones and friends; the increasing maladies – aches and pains; lonely hours that can seem endless and time that seems so fleeting; the wisdom one longs to share and the infrequency of those who seek it; the realization that death is closer while ambitions and goals of the past are not all fulfilled.

Some feel as though they were in a Soap Opera Drama – "Like Sands Through The Hourglass, So Are The Days of Our Lives." The sand all too steadily filters down – and time similarly passing all too quickly. One can reflect back to a Perry Como Lyric of many years ago:

> Magic moments, mem'ries we've been sharin'
> Magic moments, when two hearts are carin'
> Time can't erase the memory of –
> These magic moments filled with love
> The telephone call that tied up the line for hours and hours
> The Saturday dance I got up the nerve
> to send you some flowers…
> When two hearts are carin' - -
> Time can't erase the memory of,
> These magic, moments, Filled with love!

As Moses contemplated life and what needed to be accomplished, he wrote his thoughts down in Psalm 90: "Lord, you have been our dwelling place in all generations. Before the mountains were brought forth, or ever you had formed the earth and the world, from everlasting to everlasting you are God. You return man to dust…For a thousand years in your sight are but as yesterday when it is past, or as a watch in the night. You sweep them away as with a flood; they are like a dream, like grass that is renewed in the morning: in the morning it flourishes and is renewed; in the evening it fades and withers…The years of our life are seventy, or even by reason of strength eighty; yet their span is but toil and trouble; they are soon gone, and we fly away…So teach us to number our days that we may get a heart of wisdom…Have pity on your servants! Satisfy us in the morning with your steadfast love, that we may rejoice and be glad all our days. Make us glad for as many days as you have afflicted us, and for as many years as we have seen evil. Let your work be shown to your servants, and your glorious power to their children. Let the favor of the Lord our God be upon us, and establish the work of our hands upon us; yes, establish the work of our hands!"

In James 4:13-15, one is reminded: "Come now, you who say, Today or tomorrow we will go into such and such a town and spend a year there and trade and make a profit -- yet you do not know what tomorrow will bring. What is your life? For you are a mist that appears for a little time and then vanishes. Instead you ought to say, If the Lord wills, we will live and do this or that."

The Days of Our Lives – not just like Sand Seen Through The Hourglass – but also a mist, a vapor – appearing for a brief moment and then vanishing away. Like Moses, ones aim and focus should be: "So teach us to number our days that we may get a heart of wisdom…" The words of an old hymn should comfort and inspire one in the journey of life:

Never a trial that he is not there,

Never a burden that he doth not bear,
Never a sorrow that he doth not share,
Moment by moment, I'm under his care.
Moment by moment, I'm kept in his love;
Moment by moment, I've life from above;
Looking to Jesus till glory doth shine,
Moment by moment, O Lord, I am Thine.

Ones life can be lived with misery, regret, bitterness, complaint, negative perspective – or – it can be lived in the joy and comfort of the presence of the Lord; His faithful care; His strength made perfect in ones weakness; His never leaving or forsaking. Make the positive choice!

CONSIDER THESE THINGS WITH ME!

When Humpty Dumpty Begins to Fall

What can be done for a broken egg at the bottom of the wall? If that egg had some significance or notoriety, should an egg reconstructionist be found to share his expertise regarding repair of Humpty Dumpty? How can it be done – Band Aids, Super-Glue, Duct Tape? Can Humpty Dumpty be returned to his original state and status – or will he look like a patchwork quilt following his reconstruction? Does the Nursery Rhyme dismiss any hope of restoration?

> Humpty Dumpty sat on a wall;
> Humpty Dumpty had a great fall.
> All the King's horses And all the King's men
> Couldn't put Humpty together again!

A Syndicated Columnist has raised some questions about this nation as it embarked on a New Year and Decade (2001-2010). It is entitled: "A Decade Of Self-Delusion." The following resounds with pessimism: "According to the International Monetary Fund, the United States began the century producing 32 percent of the world's gross domestic product. We ended the decade producing 24 percent. No nation in modern history, save for the late Soviet Union, has seen so precipitous a decline in relative power in a single decade. The United States began the century with a budget surplus. We ended with a deficit of 10 percent of gross domestic product, which will be repeated in 2010. Where the economy was at full employment in 2000, 10 percent of the labor force is out of work today and another 7 percent is underemployed or has given up looking for a job. Between one-fourth and one-third of all U.S. manufacturing jobs have disappeared in 10 years, the fruits of a free-trade ideology that has proven anything but free for this country. Our future is being outsourced - to China. While the median income of American families was stagnant, the national debt doubled. The Dollar lost half its value against the Euro. Once the most self-sufficient republic in history, which produced 96 percent of all it consumed, the U.S.A. is almost as dependent on foreign nations today for manufactured goods, and the loans to pay for them, as we were in the early years of the republic... There are nearly 200,000 troops in Iraq and Afghanistan and another 30,000 more on the way, al-Qaeda is now in Pakistan, Yemen, Somalia and North Africa...We have a government that cannot balance its books, defend its borders or win its wars. And what is it now doing? Drafting another entitlement program as we are informed that the Social Security and Medicare trust funds have unfunded liabilities in the trillions. At the end of the first decade of the 21st century, the question is not whether we will preside over the creation of a New World Order, but whether America's decline is irreversible..."

Is this a "Humpty Dumpty" country beyond repair? Is the nation operating under a "Self-Delusion"? Should Humpty Dumpty be left at the base of the wall as a conglomeration of a fragmented shell and a scrambled yoke and egg white? If no one cares and no one tries, is that the rationale approach? It will require more than Band Aids, Super Glue and Duct Tape! One of the keys may be referencing George Washington's Prayer Book, in which he wrote: "Let my heart, therefore, gracious God, be so affected with the glory and majesty of (Thine Honor) that I may not do mine own works, but wait on Thee, and discharge those weighty duties which Thou requirest of men..." It was establishing and maintaining the focus stated in the concluding words of The Declaration of Independence:

"We, therefore, the Representatives of the United States of America, in General Congress, Assembled, appealing to Supreme Judge of the world for the rectitude of our intentions, do, in the Name, and by the Authority of the good people of these Colonies, solemnly publish and declare, That these Colonies are, and or a Right ought to be, Free and Independent States; that they are

Absolved from all Allegiance to the British Crown...And for the support of this Declaration, with a firm reliance on the protection of divine Providence, we mutually pledge to each other our Lives, our Fortunes, and our sacred Honor."

Remember the words of II Chronicles 7:14, "...if my people...will humble themselves and pray and seek my face and turn from their wicked ways - I will hear from heaven and will forgive their sin and will heal their land." Humpty Dumpty can be repaired – but – there is a price to pay and a focus required. Let's try doing it God's way!

The tendency is to avoid reality and somewhat pretend that things are not as bad as they could be. Like the picture of the ostrich with its head in the sand, life's realities are approached similarly. This is sometimes referred to as: Chutzpah and The Ugly American.

Chutzpah is a Yiddish Word meaning: "unbelievable gall; insolence; audacity." Some of the synonyms are: "insolence, impertinence, impudence - the trait of being rude and impertinent; inclined to take liberties." This idea is encapsulated in the novel – THE UGLY AMERICAN. "The 1958 novel, takes place in a fictional nation called Sarkhan (an imaginary country in Southeast Asia that somewhat resembles Burma or Thailand, but which is meant to allude to Vietnam) as its setting and includes several real people, most of whose names have been changed. The book describes the United States losing struggle against Communism because of innate arrogance and the failure to understand the local culture."

Innate Arrogance can be seen currently as a side-issue in the Health Care Provisions. It cannot be called a debate inasmuch as some people are prevented from the discussions about this major legislation. Even though most people working on this legislation have not read the 2,000 page proposal, it appears that the Senior Citizen is observed as being the major cost factor in Health Care Disbursements. Someone responded to the Senior Citizen Generation in the following:"Senior Citizens are constantly being criticized for every conceivable deficiency of the modern world, real or imaginary. We know we take responsibility for all we have done and do not blame others. However, upon reflection, we would like to point out that it was NOT the senior citizens who took:

- The MELODY out of music
- The PRIDE out of appearance
- The COURTESY out of driving
- The ROMANCE out of love
- The COMMITMENT out of marriage
- The RESPONSIBILITY out of parenthood
- The TOGETHERNESS out of the family
- The LEARNING out of education
- The SERVICE out of patriotism
- The GOLDEN RULE from rulers
- The NATIVITY SCENE out of cities
- The CIVILITY out of behavior
- The REFINEMENT out of language
- The DEDICATION out of employment
- The PRUDENCE out of spending
- The AMBITION out of achievement
- GOD out of government and school.

We certainly are NOT the ones who eliminated PATIENCE AND TOLERANCE from personal relationships and interactions with others!! We do understand THE MEANING OF PATRIOTISM, and remember those who have fought and died for our country.

In the novel, THE UGLY AMERICAN, an observation is made: "…a Burmese journalist says: For some reason, the [American] people I meet in my country are not the same as the ones I knew in the United States. A mysterious change seems to come over Americans when they go to a foreign land. They isolate themselves socially. They live pretentiously. They're loud and ostentatious. Ultimately, the phrase ugly Americans come to be applied to Americans behaving in this manner..." It's interesting how pretentious (claiming or demanding a position of distinction or merit, especially when unjustified) and unprincipled behavior surfaces when an individual enters another culture or context.

It will be interesting to see how the plight of 10 Baptist Missionaries will unfold in Haiti (February 2010). MSNBC reported yesterday: "Ten U.S. missionaries in Haiti were charged Thursday with child kidnapping and criminal association for allegedly trying to take children illegally out of the earthquake-hit country. After announcing the charges, Haitian Deputy Prosecutor Jean Ferge Joseph told the 10 their case was being sent to an investigative judge. That judge can free you but he can also continue to hold you for further proceedings, the deputy prosecutor told the five men and five women in a hearing..." The statement by the 10 is: "We didn't know what we were doing was illegal. We did not have any intention to violate the law. But now we understand it's a crime..." Romans 13:1-7 includes these words to all followers of Christ in all cultures: "Let every person be subject to the governing authorities. For there is no authority except from God, and those that exist have been instituted by God. Therefore whoever resists the authorities resists what God has appointed, and those who resist will incur judgment. For rulers are not a terror to good conduct, but too bad..." One has a responsibility to ascertain what the applicable laws are in a country or culture before an action is taken. This not debatable nor are alternative behaviors acceptable. I Peter 2:13-20 is also a reminder to be submissive to governing authorities.

The present culture has been adversely influenced and obsessed to exist without any constraints or boundaries. In many ways, we are seen and known as The Ugly American. It might also be described as our trying to get by with MOXIE AND PITHINESS. Will it be accepted and received by other nations and cultures? More and more it is being rejected in a wholesale manner.

James Perry

How can one chart a course through troubled waters and difficult times? It is always good to find someone who is gifted and skilled and can make suggestions for life that contain some humor and that are simply stated. These statements are called "Pithy Comments". Pithy means: "precisely meaningful; forceful; brief." An added bonus is if one can demonstrate "Moxie" while making the "Pithy Comment"! Moxie means: The ability to face life with spirit and courage; aggressive energy; initiative; skill; know-how." The following are Pithy & Poignant Comments by Tweety…

- Anger is a condition where the tongue works faster than the mind…
- You can't change the past but you can ruin the present by worrying over the future…
- God always gives His best to those who leave the choice with Him…
- A Hug is a great gift – one size fits all. It can be given for any occasion and it's easy to exchange…
- If anyone speaks badly of you, live so that none will believe it…
- Do what you can, for who you can with what you have and where you are…

And then – Tweety's Prayer - - -

Dear Lord, so far today I am doing alright.
I have not gossiped, lost my temper, been greedy, grumpy, nasty, selfish, or self-indulgent.
I have not whined, complained, cursed, or eaten any chocolate.
I have charged nothing on my Credit Card.
But I will be getting out of bed in a minute, and I think I will really need your help then. Amen.

The premise is: "charting a course through troubled waters and difficult times." What are a few of the Basic Biblical Guidelines for life?

Proverbs 3:5-6 (NKJV)
"Trust in the Lord with all your heart, And lean not on your own understanding; In all your ways acknowledge Him, And He shall direct your paths."

Psalm 37:4-7 (Selected: NKJV)
"Delight yourself also in the Lord, And He shall give you the desires of your heart. Commit your way to the Lord, Trust also in Him, And He shall bring it to pass…Rest in the Lord, and wait patiently for Him…"

Ephesians 4:31-32 (NKJV)
"Let all bitterness, wrath, anger, clamor, and evil speaking be put away from you, with all malice. And be kind to one another, tenderhearted, forgiving one another, just as God in Christ forgave you."

John 13:34-35 (NKJV)
"A new commandment I give to you, that you love one another; as I have loved you, that you also love one another. By this all will know that you are My disciples, if you have love for one another."

I Corinthians 13:4-8, 13 (NKJV)
"Love is patient and kind. Love is not jealous or boastful or proud or rude. Love does not demand its own way. Love is not irritable, and it keeps no record of when it has been wronged. It is never glad about injustice but rejoices whenever the truth wins out. Love never gives up, never loses faith, is always hopeful, and endures through every circumstance. Love will last forev-

er…There are three things that will endure – faith, hope, and love – and the greatest of these is love…"

Valentine's Day is observed on February 14th. Expressions of Love will be exchanged and gifts given. Let us always include and give expressions of thanks for God's Love for us, and reciprocate by sharing expressions of our Love for God! We do well to remember – Romans 5:8, "God demonstrates His own love toward us, in that while we were still sinners, Christ died for us."

CONSIDER THESE THINGS WITH ME!

Hopeless, Helpless, and Homeless

A focus upon and an appeal in behalf of Haiti rightfully continues. World Magazine for February 13th, 2010 states the following bleak estimates:– "200,000 people dead; 194,000 injured; 1 million homeless; 800,000 living in squalor and makeshift camps; 2 million needing food aid; structures destroyed – 70% in the Capitol, and 90% in towns close to the epicenter." The deplorable living conditions have continued throughout the year.

March is the normal rainy season and that will compound the plight of the helpless, hopeless and homeless. So far, the resilient people of Haiti have managed to endure and survive their many changes of government over the past 53 years.

World Magazine has this Footer in their latest publication - TRAUMATIC HISTORY:

- 1957: Voodoo physician Francois "Papa Doc" Duvalier seizes power in military coup. After his death in 1971, his son Jean-Claude "Baby Doc" takes over.
- 1986: Mounting protests force Baby Doc to seek exile in France.
- 1988: Leslie Manigat wins presidential election, but is soon ousted by military coup.
- 1990: Former Roman Catholic priest Jean-Bertrand Aristide becomes Haiti's first freely elected president.
- 1991: Aristide is ousted in a military coup that triggers a mass exodus of Haitians.
- 1993: UN Security Council approves and deploys peacekeeping mission to Haiti.
- 1994: U.S. intervention spurs the military regime to relinquish power and Aristide returns.
- 1996: René Préval becomes president.

- 1998: Hurricane Georges claims the lives of more than 400 people and wipes out 80 percent of Haiti's crops.
- 2000: Aristide wins a second presidential term.
- 2003: Voodoo becomes an official religion in Haiti.
- 2004: Violent uprisings in February sparked by allegations of election fraud force Aristide into exile; an interim rebel government takes control. In May, flooding in the south leaves more than 2,000 dead or missing.
- 2006: Préval returns as president.
- 2008: Soaring food prices incite riots in April, spurring the government to cut rice prices in an emergency move to halt unrest. Hurricanes Fay, Gustav, Hanna, and Ike strike Haiti in August-September, killing nearly 800 people and wiping out 70 percent of the country's crops. In November, faulty construction causes a Petionville school to collapse, killing nearly 100 children and adults.
- 2010: A 7.0 magnitude earthquake rocks Haiti on Jan. 12, toppling buildings and burying thousands of people in the rubble. Estimates are that more than 200,000 people may have perished.

Many appeals are made for financial assistance and one must exercise great care in how one contributes financial assistance. The two organizations that are most consistent in delivering aide and assistance in a fair and timely manner are The Salvation Army and Samaritan's Purse. A safe way to contribute is to determine whether or not the organization appealing for your finds has an ECFA Seal (Evangelical Council for Financial Accountability). One should check to determine how much of your contribution is absorbed by Administrative Costs before any is used for the designated need.

How should you approach giving to such needs? Just two thoughts and suggestions: Luke 6:38 (NLT), "If you give, you will receive. Your gift will return to you in full measure, pressed down, shaken together to make room for more, and running over.

Give as much as you can – Give generously! Whatever measure you use in giving – large or small – it will be used to measure what is given back to you." In II Corinthians 8:1-4, "Now I want to tell you…what God in his kindness has done for the needy. Though they have been going through much trouble and hard times, their wonderful joy and deep poverty have overflowed in rich generosity. For I can testify that they gave not only what they could afford but far more. And they did it of their own free will. They begged us…for the gracious privilege of sharing in the gift…" Most of us could sacrifice from our plenty - Money, Soft Drinks, Chips, Meals or Desserts for those who have nothing!

    The Associated Press Headline for Sunday - November 7, 2010 was: "HAITI VERY LUCKY AS TOMAS SKIRTED ISLAND." Hurricane Tomas pushed northward from Haiti on Saturday, leaving villagers to mop up, evacuees to return to their tents and most everyone relieved that the country did not suffer what could have been its first big disaster since the January earthquake. The storm's western track caused widespread floods, wind damage along the far edge of Haiti's coast and is blamed for the deaths of at least eight people. It was a serious blow, but far better than had been feared in a nation where storms have been known to kill thousands, and more than 1 million quake survivors were living under tarps and tents. Reports from the remote mountainous countryside and the storm's outer bands continued dropping rain on the north. Floodwaters covered streets in Leogane, the town closest to the epicenter of the January 12th quake, and about a foot of water stood on a thoroughfare of the flood-prone northwestern city of Gonaives. Mountain towns were cut off by flooded roads and landslides…But it was clear that the most-feared catastrophes were averted: Earthquake camps were not torn apart by wind, storm surge did not drown the ocean-side slums…The U.N. Office for Coordination of Humanitarian Affairs reported shortages in shelter material and other items, including rehydration salts for a cholera epidemic that officials were concerned the floods could spread. That danger remains, and medical workers were working across affected areas Saturday to contain the spread of the outbreak.

A question needs to be considered: Was Haiti Very Lucky Or Providentially Protected? The term "very lucky" defies definition. The Dictionaries do not give extensive definition to what is meant by use of the term. The World English Dictionary defines it as: "having or bringing good fortune; happening by chance." The synonyms given are: "auspicious, propitious, and favorable." Some of the Thesaurus entries given are: "advantageous... charmed... fortuitous... on a roll... holding aces... striking it rich..." On January 13, 2010 this account was given by The Associated Press: "Dazed and injured Haitians sat on darkened streets pleading for help Wednesday and untold numbers were trapped in tons of rubble brought down by the strongest earthquake to hit this poor Caribbean nation in more than 200 years.

Destroyed communications made it impossible to tell the extent of destruction from Tuesday afternoon's 7.0-magnitude tremor — or to estimate the number of dead lying among thousands of collapsed buildings in Haiti's capital of about 2 million people…Aftershocks rattled the city as women covered in dust clawed out of debris, wailing. Stunned people wandered the streets holding hands. Thousands gathered in public squares long after nightfall, singing hymns. It was clear tens of thousands lost their homes and many perished in collapsed buildings flimsy and dangerous even under normal conditions. The hospitals cannot handle all these victims…"

A concern should not be how "lucky" Haitians were regarding the anticipated Hurricane Tomas, but rather – what about the role of Providential Protection - and what has happened to all the promised aide to alleviate the tremendous health, housing and infra-structure need in the aftermath of the January 12th Earthquake. Some Christian organizations have helped considerably, whereas other entities have said they would do many things that remain to be done. One gnawing question might be: Why are more than one million people still living in Tent Cities and squalor?

It also reminds one of Basic Biblical considerations: (1) Galatians 6:9-10 instructs: "let us not grow weary of doing good, for in due season we will reap, if we do not give up. So then, as we have opportunity, let us do good to everyone, and especially to those who are of the household of faith." And (2) Ezekiel 22:29-31 exposes and warns: "The people of the land have practiced extortion and committed robbery. They have oppressed the poor and needy, and have extorted from the sojourner without justice. And I sought for a man among them who should build up the wall and stand in the breach before me for the land, that I should not destroy it, but I found none. Therefore I have poured out my indignation upon them...declares the Lord God." A worthy mantra and motto for us is: Do all the good you can; For as many as you can; For as long as you can." A summary for the nations of men is Proverbs 17:5 (NKJV), He who mocks the poor reproaches (insults) his Maker; He who is glad at calamity will not go unpunished.

CONSIDER THESE THINGS WITH ME!

Wanted - Effective Leaders

Aspiring to be a Leader is a noble goal – becoming one takes time, effort, sound core values, commitment to principles and a willingness to stand alone rather than compromise that which is right! Thomas Paine (English born American Writer whose 'Common Sense' and 'Crisis' papers were important influences on the American Revolution,1737-1809) wrote: (1) Personal - "Reputation is what men and women think of us; character is what God and angels know of us." (2) Political - "Those who want to reap the benefits of this great nation must bear the fatigue of supporting it." (3) General Principle - "'Tis the business of little minds to shrink; but he whose heart is firm, and whose conscience approves his conduct, will pursue his principles unto death." Another thought he shared is that one must - "Lead, follow, or get out of the way." Someone else noted: "Being a leader is like being a lady, if you have to go around telling people you are one, you aren't."

John Maxwell, an international Speaker and Teacher on the Subject of Leadership, tells how he was influenced early on by one who asked him: "Do You Have A Personal Plan For Growth?" As he began to reply with his work and travel schedule, he states that it became obvious – he did not have A Plan – nor did he have a clue either. John Maxwell writes: "Growth does not happen by chance. If you want to be sure to grow, you need a plan—something strategic, specific, and scheduled. Motivational speaker Earl Nightingale said, "If a person will spend one hour a day on the same subject for five years, that person will be an expert on that subject." Isn't that incredible? It shows how far we are able to go when we have the discipline to make growth our daily practice. So if you want to follow a plan, I recommend that you start by identifying an area or two in which you desire to grow, such as Leadership. Then start gathering useful resources – in print, online, on video, etc. Now your goal is to schedule learning time every day. Here's the rule of thumb I've used for years: read one book a month and digest one article/pod-cast per week... The average American adult watches close to 30 hours of television per week, with little positive return. What do you think would happen if you devoted just five of those hours to personal growth?"

Lee Iacocca wrote a book: The Nine C's of Leadership. USA Today (Reporter: James R. Healey) conducted an interview and summarized these principles:

- Curiosity - Listen to people outside the "Yes, sir" crowd. Read voraciously.
- Creative - Go out on a limb. Leadership is all about managing change.
- Communicate - You should be talking to everybody, even your enemies.
- Character - Having the guts to do the right thing. If you don't make it on character, the rest won't amount to much. (5) Courage - a commitment to sit down at the negotiation table and talk. If you're a politician, courage means taking a position even when you know it will cost you votes.
- Conviction - Fire in your belly. You've got to really want to get something done.
- Charisma - The ability to inspire. People follow a leader because they trust him or her.
- Competent - Surround yourself with people who know what they're doing. Be a problem solver.
- Common Sense - Your ability to reason."

The interview and summary concludes with this thought: "The biggest C is Crisis. Leadership is forged in times of crisis. It's easy to sit there with your feet up on the desk and talk theory, or send someone else's kids off to war when you've never seen a battlefield yourself." How does one lead during crisis times? Many flounder! Some emerge as strong leaders!

Wanted - Effective Leaders

When Jesus Christ began His earthly ministry, he immediately sought out men to Train for Leadership. He used a simple formula in Matthew 4:19, "Come, follow me...and I will make you fishers of men." His method was (a) He would Teach Them in terms of Sound Principles, and (b) He would Model for them what a Leader must be (John 13, where Jesus takes the role of a servant and washes the disciples' feet is an illustration of this). The Model factor indicates that Leadership and Disciple Ministry is "more caught than taught." There were obvious truths they needed to learn but there were necessary behaviors and ministry they needed to observe. Some display what seems like innate Leadership Skills, but anyone who finds himself/herself in a Leadership role must have those innate skills harnessed and honed. Are you a Leader? Who or What are you following? Do their core values mesh with yours?

Many times, a person gifted in public speaking and who is charismatic in personality can influence others in such a way that they will conclude such a person will be a great leader. A person skilled in the English Language can speak in such ways that no clear, precise or definitive discourse occurs. The person has learned how to Finesse A Blunder or any other situation that may come into play.

Finesse means: "Refinement and delicacy of performance, execution... Skillful, subtle handling of a situation; tactful, diplomatic maneuvering... To handle with a deceptive or evasive strategy..." Much political speech performs in this capacity. Rarely does one hear a precise answer to a specific question or interrogatory. The other approach is to control who will be involved in posing a question. This will prevent anything confrontational or deliberative from transpiring. This is all too common in the area of political discourse. Very few men or women will respond with a direct "yes" or "no". In the process of the response, the question is often reframed and response is given to the reframed proposition.

An illustration of control in a story of some interest is described by The Associated Press when the Tiger Woods incident occurred. Tiger Woods had been championed as a role model and a person of exemplary character. Suddenly, the unthinkable occurred and sordid details began to be known. A Golf icon was now blemished. Endorsements and sponsorships were terminated. As February 2010 unfolded, the press developed this scenario: "Out of sight for almost three months, Tiger Woods will be back for a day. After that — who knows. Golf's biggest star is to make his first public appearance Friday since he ran his SUV over a fire hydrant and into a tree outside his Florida home on November 27, 2009 setting off a shocking and sordid sex scandal. The setting for his return is decidedly friendly. It may be hard to remember the planet is watching. Woods will speak to a small group of 'friends, colleagues and close associates' in the Sunset Room on the second floor of the TPC Sawgrass, home of the PGA Tour. Just one video camera will broadcast the event and there will be no questions. Once he's done, Woods apparently won't be sticking around much longer. He is to return to therapy after he speaks about his infidelity and his future plans, according to a letter from PGA Tour commissioner Tim Finchem obtained by The Associated Press." It has been suggested that someone else has crafted the remarks that will be given.

It would be beneficial for any therapy if there was just a simple and plain statement of admission. Why not say: "I made some foolish and selfish choices that have affected and hurt those who are the closest to me – my wife and children. I have tried to cover up my affairs and accident but I want to state plainly that I have been wrong for doing the things I have done. I don't deserve understanding or forgiveness but I hope that my wife and children can find the mercy and compassion to forgive me for my inappropriate and egregious behavior. The many people who have followed my career and been so helpful to me – I hope that they too will find it possible to grant me a second chance. I wish there was a way for me to adequately make amends – I will try my best to be more responsible and honorable in the future..." This is the best one could hope for from a secular-oriented sports professional and business man.

Innately, everyone has a tendency to avoid and/or sugar-coat the truth. The Garden of Eden is a classic example of an act of disobedience – and – two individuals thinking they could hide their act and themselves from Almighty God. Adam and Eve set in motion this process of Finessing A Blunder/Sin.

A classic Biblical example is when David allowed himself to lust for Bathsheba. II Samuel 11-12 tells the sad story of King David and his adultery with Bathsheba. A complication develops when Bathsheba becomes pregnant. In his attempt to cover-up his sinful behavior, King David tries to manipulate Uriah – the husband of Bathsheba by bringing him home for a brief furlough from a battle. When this fails, Kind David continues in his Finessing A Blunder/Sin by ordering that Uriah be allowed to be killed in Battle. This takes place and King David believed his cover-up worked effectively and efficiently.

One thing King David allowed himself to forget – – God! When he remembers God, all Finessing Of A Blunder/Sin comes to a screeching halt. David writes: "Blessed is he whose transgressions are forgiven ...When I kept silent (about my sin), my bones wasted away through my groaning all day long...I acknowledged my sin to you and did not cover up my iniquity. I said, I will confess my transgressions to the Lord-- and you forgave the guilt of my sin" (Psalm 32:1-5). "Have mercy on me, O God, according to your unfailing love; according to your great compassion blot out my transgressions. Wash away all my iniquity and cleanse me from my sin. For I know my transgressions, and my sin is always before me. Against you, you only, have I sinned and done what is evil in your sight" (Psalm 51:1-4). Do you try to Finesse your Blunders/Sins? Acknowledge them and know God's cleansing and forgiveness. Don't Delay – Do It Today!

The desire to Finesse A Blunder or to deceive occurs frequently. However, those who are deemed to be effective leaders are not always the most scrupulous. They set out to achieve an agenda by fair means or foul. One who had been elected by her peers to be Speaker of the House of Representatives from 2006 through 2010 was Nancy Pelosi.

Nancy Pelosi gave a statement of determination near the end of January 2010 regarding Health Care when she said: "We'll go through the gate. If the gate's closed, we'll go over the fence. If the fence is too high, we'll pole-vault in. If that doesn't work, we'll parachute in." Determination can be a very good thing when it comes to promoting what is right and good, but it can become a means where the wrong and bad occur when it promotes a cause that could easily bankrupt the government, businesses and the citizenry. Determination is an interesting word. It means: "the act of making or arriving at a decision; firmness of purpose; resolve; a fixed intention or resolution; the decision or settlement arrived at or pronounced…" A critique, one that is a bit caustic of this bold statement, was expressed by The American Voice: "Wow! - did not know she possessed athletic prowess. Talk about hyperbole!! Nancy, you mean like you did this last year? Will this event be televised on CSPAN? Or, is this a private event behind closed doors of the White House?"

It makes one think of Mary Poppins when Julie Andrews came floating in with her Parasol in hand. The Mary Poppins film focuses on children who need a Nanny to provide them with strict care. "The latest nanny, Katie Nanna, quits out of exasperation after the children, Jane and Michael run off in pursuit of a wayward kite. The children are reported missing. A policeman arrives with the children, who ask their father to help repair their damaged kite. The father dismisses them and advertises for an authoritarian nanny-replacement. The children draft their own advertisement asking for a fun, kind-hearted and caring person, but their father tears up the paper and throws it in the fireplace. Unnoticed, the note's remains float up the chimney. The next day there is a queue of old and disagreeable nanny candidates waiting at the door. However, a strong gust of wind literally blows the queue away, and Mary Poppins floats down with her umbrella in hand to apply. The father is stunned to see that this calmly defiant new nanny has responded to the children's ad despite the fact he destroyed it. As he puzzles, Mary Poppins employs herself and begins work. The children face surprises of their own: Mary possesses a bottomless carpetbag, and makes contents of the children's nursery come to life and tidy themselves by snapping her fingers..." Perhaps Nanny Nancy considers herself to be calmly defiant - a reincarnation of Mary Poppins who can float over the wall of opposition with her umbrella in hand – along with her Health Care Proposal - snap her fingers and make inanimate things become animate. Nanny Nancy may prevail with her minions believing that the citizenry wants what they have repeatedly said they don't want. The clue for Nanny Nancy is that the citizenry wants "Reform" – not – "Replacement"! They want "Cost Containment" – not – "Cost Escalation"! The People want "Tort Reform" – not – Tort Revisionism"! There are not enough "Parachutes, Poles for Vaulting or Parasols" to get the citizenry to float over the wall with Nanny Nancy.

    People have often referred to the statement by Edmund Burke: "All that is necessary for evil to triumph is for all good men to do nothing." However, the acceptable Biblical concept is: When good men do nothing, they get nothing good done.

    Two places in particular state the Christian Principle and Profile for doing good in this world and culture.

Galatians 6:9-10 "Let us not become weary in doing good, for at the proper time we will reap a harvest if we do not give up. Therefore, as we have opportunity, let us do good to all people, especially to those who belong to the family of believers..."

Titus 2:11-14 (selected) "For the grace of God that brings salvation has appeared to all men. It teaches us to say – No! - to ungodliness and worldly passions, and to live self-controlled, upright and godly lives…while we wait for the blessed hope--the glorious appearing of our great God and Savior, Jesus Christ, who gave himself for us to redeem us from all wickedness and to purify for himself a people that are his very own, eager to do what is good."

We don't need Parachutes, Pole Vaults or Parasols – just consistency and faithfulness in doing what Jesus Christ modeled and taught. There is no discrimination when one loves his neighbor as himself; and loves his enemy and does good to those who misuse and abuse him. It's a radical approach to life but it is also a Biblical lesson that must be learned and demonstrated.

Have you ever thought about yourself as a leader? Are you willing to be God's Man or Woman to be used by Him as He sees fit? Are you willing to go anywhere, at any time, to do any work and at any cost if it is God's Will and Purpose for your life.

As Paul writes his epistle to the Colossians, he mentions one who is known to be a Leader-Pastor for the people and the Church. Note his words in Colossians 4:12-13 (NKJV), "Epaphras, who is one of you, a bondservant of Christ, greets you, always laboring fervently for you in prayers, that you may stand perfect and complete in all the will of God. For I bear him witness that he has a great zeal for you…" In The Message Paraphrase, these words are rendered: "Epaphras, who is one of you, says hello. What a trooper he has been! He's been tireless in his prayers for you, praying that you'll stand firm, mature and confident in everything God wants you to do. I've watched him closely, and can report on how hard he has worked for you…"

Are you ready to consider what God wants you to do for Him? Are you ready to fit your life into His plan for you?

CONSIDER THESE THINGS WITH ME!

Virtuous Vacillations

Foundational Principles and Moral Imperatives should never be compromised or ignored. This is especially vital when it pertains to those who govern and those who are governed. To be virtuous means: "conforming to moral and ethical principles; being morally excellent; upright..." Whereas, vacillation means: "To swing indecisively from one course of action or opinion to another..."

An example of this can be seen in the government focus over the past year regarding the passage of Health Care Reform. When he was a candidate, the President stated on different occasions:

CBS Interview 11/2/04
- My understanding of the Senate is that you need 60 votes to get something significant to happen, which means that Democrats and Republicans have to ask the question, do we have the will to move an American agenda forward, not a Democratic or Republican agenda forward?

Center for American Progress Conference 7/12/06
- Those big-ticket items: fixing our health care system...one of the arguments that sometimes I get with my fellow progressives...is this notion that we should function...where we get a fifty plus one victory...If we want to transform the country, though, that requires a sizeable majority.

Change to Win Convention 9/25/07
- The bottom line is that our healthcare plans are similar, the question once again is, who can get it done? Who can build a movement for change? We're going to have to

have a majority to get a bill to my desk. That is not just a fifty plus one majority.

President Obama Interview - the Concord Monitor 10/9/07
- You've got to break out of what I call the sort of fifty plus one pattern of presidential politics. Maybe you eke out a victory of fifty plus one. Then you can't govern…We are not going to pass universal health care with a fifty plus one strategy.

In March 2010, the President said:
- "No matter which approach you favor, I believe the United States Congress owes the American people a final vote on health care reform. We have debated this issue thoroughly, not just for a year, but for decades. Reform has already passed the House with a majority. It has already passed the Senate with a super-majority of sixty votes. And now it deserves the same kind of up-or-down vote that was cast on welfare reform, the Children's Health Insurance Program, COBRA health coverage for the unemployed, and both Bush tax cuts -- all of which had to pass Congress with nothing more than a simple majority (implying: 51 votes)…"

Some of the Founding Principles which have been forgotten by the current generation are ideas shared by Thomas Jefferson: (1) "The democracy will cease to exist when you take away from those who are willing to work and give to those who would not;" (2) "It is incumbent on every generation to pay its own debts as it goes. A principle which if acted on would save one-half the wars of the world;" and (3) "I predict future happiness for Americans if they can prevent the government from wasting the labors of the people under the pretense of taking care of them."

Is this oxymoron – virtuous vacillation – acceptable in any area of life? In the Sermon on the Mount, Jesus stated this Foundational Principle and Moral Imperative – Matthew 5:33-37 – "you have heard that it was said to the people long ago, Do not break your oath, but keep the oaths you have made to the Lord. But I tell you, Do not swear at all: either by heaven, for it is God's throne; or by the earth, for it is His footstool…Simply let your Yes, be Yes, and your No, No; anything beyond this comes from the evil one." It is basically (a) have scruples (a moral or ethical consideration or standard that acts as a restraining force or inhibits certain actions), (b) demonstrate consistency, and (c) be a person of character and integrity! These are values that should never be compromised or forgotten!

The broad stroke approach is that a government and/or an individual must have a goal. The question that is seldom asked in government is: In the effort to focus on a goal and trying to achieve it, are we Aiming or Maiming in the process.

We are all aware of the trite saying that states: "If You Aim At Nothing – You Will Always Hit Your Target!" Another paraphrased saying is: If you throw enough Jell-O at a wall – some will eventually stick – but there'll be a terrible mess as a result of that effort. Taking "aim" always suggests precision and direction. A well-aimed rifle shot is much better than a random shotgun blast. One will hit the target – the other can result in damage and maiming. The more one takes specific aim with the skill of a marksman the more likely the target and goal will be achieved. It accomplishes a level of confidence as one hones the skill of accurate aim and marksmanship.

A New Confidence Index has been released. "For 44 years, since 1966, The Harris Poll has measured how confident Americans are in the leaders of major U.S. institutions. Then, based on the responses, Harris calculates an overall Confidence Index. Over the years, it has gone up and down. In 2002, it touched 65. In 2008, it fell to 44. This year, it stands at 53, one point lower than in early 2009. While the overall Confidence Index has not shifted much this year, the individual confidence ratings used to calculate this average have undergone a great deal of change. The biggest modulation since early 2009 is the substantial drop in public confidence in the White House. The number of those with a great deal of confidence has fallen by 9 points from 36% to 27%. There have also been declines in those with a great deal of confidence in colleges and universities (from 40% to 35%), organized religion (from 30% to 26%) and television news (from 22% to 17%). On the other hand, there have been increases in the number of those with a "great deal of confidence" in the courts and justice system (from 19% to 24%), major companies (from 11% to 15%) and Congress (from 4% to 8%). However, confidence in all of these institutions is still very low. The five top institutions that inspire a great deal of confidence in more than 30 percent of Americans include the military (59%), small businesses (50%), major educational institutions, such as colleges and universities (35%), medicine (34%) and the U.S. Supreme Court (31%).The five least inspirational institutions include organized labor (14%), the press (13%), law firms (13%), Congress (8%) and Wall Street (8%)."

Most of these findings are based on two primary areas: (1) perception – the influences that impact how one thinks things are going and/or happening; and (2) result – does one have the sense that things are occurring in an even-handed way with maximum integrity. The media and political spin can have an effect upon how one thinks, as well as the level of confidence one has at a given point. Usually, one looks for a light at the end of the tunnel. Currently, most people can't even find the tunnel much less any light at the end of it. The current political climate was based on the premise of: "Change You Can Believe In" and "Hope" for those who are struggling and laden with despair of ever having a portion of the American Dream. While those political slogans can (and did) gain attention and response, it is always a misdirection for the poor, needy, desperate and hopeless. The misdirection is putting ones confidence in a man, a party, political promises and rhetoric, etc. When realization and relief do not appear on one's horizon, a person becomes mentally maimed - and disillusioned.

Once more, the aim was to gain votes – not to provide assistance and relief.

What can one do? The obvious answer is to change the focus. Don't rely on rhetoric, hollow promises or a man's style. The true confidence one should have is stated in – Psalm 146:3-5 – "Do not put your trust in princes, in a son of man, in whom there is no salvation. When his breath departs, he returns to the earth; on that very day his plans perish. Blessed is he whose help and whose hope is in the Lord his God," In Hebrews 10:35-36, "…do not throw away your confidence, which has a great reward. For you have need of endurance, so that when you have done the will of God you may receive what is promised." Placing ones hopes and confidence in a man or movement will allow one to soon reach a place where there is a loss of trust and confidence in everyone and everything. Putting ones hopes, dreams, aspirations and confidence in the Lord will always result in fulfillment, acceptance, peace and assurance because God's Aim is precise – He always hits the correct target at the right moment. He will never Maim you physically or spiritually. He will always guard your mind, will and emotions. You can always confidently rely upon Him.

Vince Lombardi was a great football coach with the Green Bay Packers from the late 1950s through the 1960s and had a rallying statement that he used frequently with his teams and players that placed emphasis upon winning, namely, "Winning isn't everything – it is the only thing!"

Wikipedia has this statement: "The quotation is widely attributed to American football coach Vince Lombardi, who is on record using the quotation as early as 1959 in his opening talk on the first day of the Packers' training camp. The quotation captured the American public's attention during Lombardi's highly successful reign as coach of the Packers in the 1960s. Over time, the quotation took on a life of its own. The words graced the walls of locker rooms, ignited pre-game pep talks, and echoed from the rafters of banquet halls. According to the late James

Michener's Sports in America, Lombardi claimed to have been misquoted. What he intended to say was "Winning isn't everything. The will to win is the only thing!" That's a good thought – "the will to win is the only thing!"

For the follower of the Lord Jesus Christ, we have a very clear and profound statement regarding Victory in Christ. The words are in Romans 8:31-39 (ESV Selected): "What then shall we say to these things? If God is for us, who can be against us? He who did not spare his own Son but gave him up for us all, how will he not also with him graciously give us all things? Who shall bring any charge against God's elect? It is God who justifies. Who is to condemn? Christ Jesus is the one who died--more than that, who was raised--who is at the right hand of God, who indeed is interceding for us. Who shall separate us from the love of Christ? Shall tribulation, or distress, or persecution, or famine, or nakedness, or danger, or sword?

"No, in all these things we are more than conquerors through him who loved us. For I am sure that neither death nor life, nor angels nor rulers, nor things present nor things to come, nor powers, nor height nor depth, nor anything else in all creation, will be able to separate us from the love of God in Christ Jesus our Lord."

Politicians do not always transact the people's business on a level playing field. To win at any cost is not a mark of integrity or character.

In the Christian's life, one needs to guard his/her integrity and character so that it is never compromised in any way. If we yield to the course of least resistance and allow for compromise, we allow ourselves to lose the joy, peace, and confidence in one's daily walk.

The words written in 1939 by E.M. Bartlett contain the great truth of the work of Jesus Christ in our behalf.

> I heard an old, old story, How a Savior came from glory,
> How He gave His life on Calvary

To save a wretch like me;
I heard about His groaning,
Of His precious blood's atoning,
Then I repented of my sins And won the victory.

CONSIDER THESE THINGS WITH ME!

Life, Liberty and the Pursuit of. . .

Many years ago, a group of men who were willing to risk their lives and fortunes to establish a nation that would be free from the avarice (insatiable greed for riches; inordinate, miserly desire to gain and hoard wealth) and tyranny of men, penned the words (In Congress, July 4, 1776 - The Unanimous Declaration of the Thirteen United States of America): "When in the Course of human events it becomes necessary for one people to dissolve the political bands which have connected them with another and to assume among the powers of the earth, the separate and equal station to which the Laws of Nature and of Nature's God entitle them, a decent respect to the opinions of mankind requires that they should declare the causes which impel them to the separation. We hold these truths to be self-evident, that all men are created equal, that they are endowed by their Creator with certain unalienable Rights, that among these are Life, Liberty and the pursuit of Happiness. — That to secure these rights, Governments are instituted among Men, deriving their just powers from the consent of the governed, — That whenever any Form of Government becomes destructive of these ends, it is the Right of the People to alter or to abolish it, and to institute new Government, laying its foundation on such principles and organizing its powers in such form, as to them shall seem most likely to effect their Safety and Happiness…"

Today, after 234 years, how is this Pursuit working out? Is the Government truly "of the people, for the people, by the people…"? How does one become like a mere pawn and relegated to insignificance? Do you feel and believe that The Government today is actually concerned for you and your need, or might there be a more sinister motive, namely, their personal career and fortunes? How do people and governments get to this point of inward focus and personal interests?

Perhaps we can glean an insight and answer from the Book: THE CHOICE by Max Lucado, where we read: "…Unbound by today, God and the angel walked into the realm of tomorrow. There, see the fruit of the seed of choice, both the sweet and the bitter. The angel gasped at what he saw. Spontaneous love. Voluntary devotion. Chosen tenderness. Never had he seen anything like these. He felt the love of the Adams. He heard the joy of Eve and her daughters. He saw the food and the burdens shared. He absorbed the kindness and marveled at the warmth.

Heaven has never seen such beauty, my Lord. Truly, this is your greatest creation.

Ah, but you've only seen the sweet. Now witness the bitter.

A stench enveloped the pair.

The angel turned in horror and proclaimed, What is it? The Creator spoke only one word: SELFISHNESS.

The angel stood speechless as they passed through centuries of repugnance. Never had he seen such filth. Rotten hearts. Ruptured promises. Forgotten loyalties. Children of the creation wandering blindly in lonely labyrinths.

This is the result of choice? the angel asked. Yes.

They will forget you? Yes.

They will reject you? Yes.

They will never come back? Some will. Most won't.

What will it take to make them listen?

The Creator walked on in time, further and further into the future, until he stood by a tree. A tree that would be fashioned into a cradle. Even then he could smell the hay that would surround him. With another step into the future, He paused before another tree. It stood alone, a stubborn ruler of a bald hill. The trunk was thick, and the wood was strong. Soon it would be cut. Soon it would be trimmed. Soon it would be mounted on the stony brow of another hill. And soon He would be hung on it…"

Life, Liberty and the Pursuit of. . .

Has Max Lucado defined the issue for us – selfishness and self-centered interests? Is that why Life, Liberty and the Pursuit of Happiness seems to elude so many? In Luke 9:23-25, Jesus sets the parameters for following Him, and asks a poignant rhetorical question. We read: "Jesus said to them all: If anyone would come after me, he must deny himself and take up his cross daily and follow Me. For whoever wants to save his life will lose it, but whoever loses his life for Me will save it. What good is it for a man to gain the whole world, and yet lose or forfeit his very self?" Selfishness - self-centered interests – must be sacrificed on that cross. We are here to emulate the Savior and Creator! One needs to love God and to show God-Love to all. God-Love gave us Jesus and Redemption!

As one observes life unfolding in day by day experiences, it is apparent that many function with a major dose of Unmitigated Gall. It is difficult to understand how gullibility and naiveté can be so common - that it can be observed about otherwise astute and intelligent people. When listening to public addresses and discussion, one has a sense there is something wrong with what is being said - - it just doesn't sound logical or reasonable.

For instance, in contemporary social matters, a Health Reform Bill that has not been openly discussed, or publicly read, or voted upon – people are lined up on either side either for or against it. Then – a deadline is set for the Congress to vote for it so it can be signed into Law – with the hope and promise that corrections and amendments will quickly be made to it.

Mind-boggling? Yes!
Incredulous? Absolutely!
Illogical? Indeed!

This is where the unmitigated gall surfaces as the reality! There is only one expression that can summarize such activity and behavior – Shameful!

There is an excellent Book Review submitted by David Mays: "The Speed of Trust – The One Thing That Changes Everything by Stephen M. R. Covey. David Mays review includes these thoughts: "This book surveys four core constituents of trust: integrity, intent, capability, and results. All four are needed to engender trust in relationships, organizations, and society. With trust, everything runs faster, smoother and cheaper. A lack of trust imposes a "tax" in speed and costs. Covey outlines 13 steps to see, speak, and behave in ways that build trust. "The ability to establish, grow, extend, and restore trust with all stakeholders--customers, business partners, investors, and co-workers--is the key leadership competency of the new global economy."

The body of the review includes these thoughts and comments: "Whether you're on a sports team, in an office or a member of a family, if you can't trust one another there's going to be trouble", Joe Paterno.

The Sarbanes-Oxley Act is intended to prevent corporate scandals like WorldCom and Enron. The cost of implementing one part of it is estimated at $35 billion. This amounts to a huge "tax" resulting from a loss of trust in corporate institutions. Some leading organizations ask their employees directly; Do you trust your boss? This may be the most predictive indicator of team performance…Trust is one of the most powerful forms of motivation and inspiration. Who trusts you? Trust is a function of character and competence. Covey deals with five circles, or waves, of trust: trust in yourself (confidence in ourselves, our ability to set and achieve goals), in relationships, in organizations, in the market (your brand reputation), and in society (creating value for others). Leadership is getting results in a way that inspires trust. The means are as important as the ends.

The First Wave - Self Trust. The Principle of Credibility The foundational principle is credibility or believability. Am I believable? Do I trust myself? And Am I someone others can trust? The four cores are:

1. <u>INTEGRITY: HONESTY</u>, integratedness, being congruent inside and out, acting our values and beliefs. Are you congruent? "Rules cannot take the place of character." Alan Greenspan

2. <u>INTENT:</u> our motives, agenda, and resulting behavior - What's your agenda? Intent matters. It grows out of character. Examine your own motives. Am I seeking to bless or impress?

3. <u>CAPABILITIES:</u> talents, attitudes, skills, knowledge, and style - Are you relevant? "Our capability to do the task at hand inspires trust in others."

4. <u>RESULTS:</u> our track record, performance, getting the right things done - What's your track record? Results make you credible and establish trust."

The basic goal and commitment for the follower of Jesus Christ is:

(a) II Corinthians 8:21, "For we are taking pains to do what is right, not only in the eyes of the Lord but also in the eyes of men.",

(b) Romans 12:17-18, "Be careful to do what is right in the eyes of everybody. If it is possible, as far as it depends on you, live at peace with everyone.", and

(c) I Peter 3:16, "keeping a clear conscience, so that those who speak maliciously against your good behavior in Christ may be ashamed of their slander."

This is the minimum standard and an important starting point! Is this the level of your commitment to The One Who loved you and gave Himself for you? It should be! You'll be glad you took this step in and for your life.

CONSIDER THESE THINGS WITH ME!

Insulting More Than Intelligence

Do you ever get weary of the "News" and "Commentary" (that is becoming more and more predictable and boring)? Do you ever wish or pray that the Members of Congress would get real jobs and quit tampering with the Constitution and our lives? Have you come to a place where everything seems to be more topsy-turvy than practical and functional? Do you really believe that Government is looking out for you and generations that will follow? Do you wish you had a remote or button where you could push it and turn off all of this talk and convoluted (twisted; complicated; intricately involved) change of direction in our nation? Do you have an increasing sense that those who govern have crossed a line where they are insulting more than your intelligence by what they propose and enact?

Insults are a type of art-form. If one was to reciprocate in terms of the mish-mash being sent our way day after day, maybe some of the following would apply. These are taken from a list entitled: When Insults Had Class (from an era before the English Language was boiled down to four-letter words):

- The exchange between Churchill & Lady Astor: She said, "If you were my husband I'd give you poison." He said, "If you were my wife, I'd drink it."
- "He has all the virtues I dislike and none of the vices I admire." - Winston Churchill
- "I have never killed a man, but I have read many obituaries with great pleasure." Clarence Darrow
- "He has never been known to use a word that might send a reader to the dictionary." William Faulkner (about Ernest Hemingway).
- "I didn't attend the funeral, but I sent a nice letter saying I approved of it." Mark Twain

- "He has no enemies, but is intensely disliked by his friends." Oscar Wilde
- "I've just learned about his illness. Let's hope it's nothing trivial." Irvin S. Cobb
- "Why do you sit there looking like an envelope without any address on it?" Mark Twain
- "Some cause happiness wherever they go; others, whenever they go." Oscar Wilde
- "He uses statistics as a drunken man uses lamp-post - for support rather than illumination." Andrew Lang
- "I've had a perfectly wonderful evening. But this wasn't it." Groucho Marx
- "I am enclosing two tickets to the first night of my new play; bring a friend, if you have one." George Bernard Shaw to Winston Churchill
- "Cannot possibly attend first night, will attend second, if there is one." Winston Churchill, in response.
- "I feel so miserable without you; it's almost like having you here." Stephen Bishop

Words should always be chosen carefully and used wisely; words can either destroy or build up. When God said: "let there be…", the world and everything in it was created. In human discourse, words can impact another or cause one to ignore the speaker. The Wisdom Literature of the Old Testament contains these axioms for life. Proverbs 13:3, "He who guards his lips guards his life, but he who speaks rashly will come to ruin." Ecclesiastes 5:1-2, "Guard your steps when you go to the house of God. Go near to listen rather than to offer the sacrifice of fools, who do not know that they do wrong. Do not be quick with your mouth, do not be hasty in your heart to utter anything before God. God is in heaven and you are on earth, so let your words be few." This guideline for worship is also valuable and useful in terms of ones discourse in the secular world. There is another important application in James 1:19-22, "…take note of this: Everyone should be quick to listen, slow to speak and slow to become angry, for man's anger does not bring about the righteous life that God desires. Therefore, get rid of all moral filth and the evil that is so prevalent and humbly accept the word (God's Word) planted in you, which can save you. Do not merely listen to the word, and so deceive yourselves. Do what it says." Much of the Bible was written out of a secular context of hardship and persecution. In spite of those who would not only insult ones intelligence but also inflict personal and bodily harm, the Lord continually reminded His own that He would always be faithful - providing for and sustaining His people. He and His promises are never-changing. Man flip-flops all over the place – God never does. Trust Him and be at peace in Him!

Even though these truths are available and useful for us, we sometimes find ourselves in the doldrums with the sense that we can't win for losing. The phrase "Can't Win For Losing" is a common one employed when best efforts are either frustrated and/or fail to accomplish the desired ends. It is not primarily focusing upon the Health Care Reform issues or 2010, or Tea Party Movements, or an analysis that leads one to believe Capitalism is lost and Socialism has replaced it. When frustrated and feeling helpless, a person may shrug and exclaim: "I Just Can't Win for Losing!" Politically – one might feel that way - but there is more to life, culture and the world than just American Politics and Posturing.

Consider this news item and headline: "Invasion of the Grasshoppers" or "Day of the Grasshopper Looms"! The Wall Street Journal in a March 28th, 2010 item states: "Farmers and ranchers across the West are bracing for a grasshopper infestation that could devastate millions of acres of crops and land used for grazing. Over the coming weeks, federal officials say, grasshoppers will likely hatch in bigger numbers than any year since 1985. Hungry swarms caused hundreds of millions of dollars in damage that year when they devoured corn, barley, alfalfa, beets - even fence posts and the paint off the sides of barns…A federal survey of 17 States taken last fall found critically high numbers of adult grasshoppers in parts of Idaho, Montana, Nebraska, South Dakota and Wyoming. Each mature female lays hundreds of eggs. So the population could be very, very high this year...Grasshoppers, which typically thrive in the west at densities of about eight mature insects per square yard, are a healthy part of the ecosystem - and food for birds such as the sage grouse. But last fall, surveys found 15 per square yard in hot spots, and those numbers are expected to rise this summer. Peak infestation areas can easily hit 60 or more hungry hoppers per square yard - a population so dense that they swarm over every surface on passing cars, cover country roads like a rug and lie so thick on grassy patches. To try to get ahead of the problem, Wyoming has allocated $2.7 million for suppression efforts, including aerial spraying of the pesticide Dimilin, which is fatal to maturing grasshoppers..."

For those desiring to provide for themselves, the Grasshopper-Locust issue is an added frustration. This is especially true when one reads another Headline: "CBO report: Debt will rise to 90% of GDP." One becomes dismayed when reading: "The Fiscal 2011 budget will generate nearly $10 trillion in cumulative budget deficits over the next 10 years, $1.2 trillion more than originally projected, and raise the federal debt to 90% of the nation's economic output by 2020, the Congressional Budget Office reported Thursday." It gives little comfort to know: "The Federal Public Debt, which was $6.3 trillion ($56,000 per household at the start of 2009), totals $8.2 trillion ($72,000 per household) today, and it's headed toward $20.3 trillion (more than $170,000 per household) in 2020, according to CBO's deficit estimates. That figure would equal 90% of the estimated gross domestic product in 2020, up from 40% at the end of fiscal 2008. By comparison, America's debt-to-GDP ratio peaked at 109% at the end of World War II, while the ratio for economically troubled Greece hit 115% last year."

One wonders if a Headline in the non-too-distant future might appear about this nation: O, How The Mighty Have Fallen!

Insulting More Than Intelligence

What should one do if a plague of grasshoppers comes upon a portion of the nation? What can one do if the nation bankrupts itself – and effectively loses prestige and power in the world? Must one be relegated to those who feel helpless and frustrated, and exclaim with them: "I Just Can't Win For Losing!"? Perhaps we should learn from a Prophet of God who faced similar challenges. In Habakkuk 3:17-19, a day of great calamity and after Habakkuk had asked the Lord for the answer to the personal and national plight, he comes to this conclusion: "Though the fig tree does not bud and there are no grapes on the vines, though the olive crop fails and the fields produce no food, though there are no sheep in the pen and no cattle in the stalls, yet I will rejoice in the Lord, I will be joyful in God my Savior. The Sovereign Lord is my strength; he makes my feet like the feet of a deer, he enables me to go on the heights." It may take desperate times to get people to redirect their priorities and focus toward God, and God Alone. There is still time to do this – but – it needs to be done soon - now!

In the first chapter of The Purpose Driven Life is the important statement: "It All Starts with God -It's not about you. The purpose of your life is far greater than your own personal fulfillment, your peace of mind, or even your happiness. It's far greater than your family, your career, or even your wildest dreams and ambitions. If you want to know why you were placed on this planet, you must begin with God. You were born by his purpose and for his purpose."

There is a very inspiring Contemporary Christian song that summarizes that thought:

>God and God alone
>created all these things we call our own
>From the mighty to the small
>the Glory in them all
>is God's and God's alone.
>God and God alone

is fit to take the universe's throne
Let everything that lives
reserve it's truest praise for
God and God alone.

God and God alone
reveals the truth of all we call unknown
and the best and worst of man
wont change the Master's plan it's
God's and God's alone.

God and God alone
will be the joy of our eternal home
He will be our one desire
Our hearts will never tire of
God's and God's alone.

CONSIDER THESE THINGS WITH ME!

A Man's Word is His Bond (Or Is It?)

A phrase attributed to Miguel de Cervantes is: "An honest man's word is as good as his bond." This was a standard in the early days of our nation. It continues as an innate readiness for many today. Somewhere along the way, Situational Ethics was introduced and accepted as a reasonable lifestyle and the Philosophy that the end justifies the means was embraced. This is a very old phrase dating back and attributed to "The Greek playwright Sophocles who wrote in Electra (c 409 B.C.), 'The end excuses any evil,' a thought later rendered by the Roman poet Ovid as 'The result justifies the deed' in 'Heroides' (c. 10 B.C.)." [From "Wise Words and Wives' Tales: The Origins, Meanings and Time-Honored Wisdom of Proverbs and Folk Sayings Olde and New" by Stuart Flexner and Doris Flexner, Avon Books, New York, 1993].

If we fast-forward to our world today, how reliable is a man's word? Can it be received and accepted as one saying what he means and meaning what he says? If a person swears to "tell the truth, the whole truth, and nothing but the truth – so help me God!", shouldn't that mean that what is spoken will be precise, exact and honest? The following was publicly stated some time ago: "The way to make government responsible is to hold it accountable and the way to hold it accountable is to make it transparent so that the American people can know exactly what decisions are being made, how they are being made and whether their interests are being well-served. The directives I am giving my administration today on how to interpret the Freedom of Information Act will do just that. For a long time now, there has been too much secrecy in this city. The old rules said that if there was a defensible argument for not disclosing something to the American people, then it should not be disclosed. That era is now over. Starting today, every agency and department should know that this administration stands on the side not of those who seek to withhold information, but those who seek to make it known...the mere fact that you have the legal power to keep something secret doesn't mean you should always use it." These are the words of President Obama in 2009. However, The Associated Press has reported the following: "When President Obama took office, he famously aspired to be the leader in administrative transparency, but now he finds himself struggling to enforce it within his own government. In fiscal year 2009, 17 major governmental agencies refused to release information, claiming legal exemptions, 466,872 times, an increase of nearly 50 percent from the previous year...In 2008, the government refused 312,683 requests made under the Freedom of Information Act..."

Being President of anything is in and of itself daunting and challenging at the very least! That being said, keeping one's word should be as natural as breathing! Ecclesiastes 5:1-6 (NLT) reminds one what is acceptable before and in the Presence of God. "As you enter the house of God, keep your ears open and your mouth shut! Don't be a fool who doesn't realize that mindless offerings to God are evil. And don't make rash promises to God, for he is in heaven, and you are only here on earth. So let your words be few. Just as being too busy gives you nightmares, being a fool makes you a blabbermouth. So when you make a promise to God, don't delay in following through, for God takes no pleasure in fools. Keep all the promises you make to him. It is better to say nothing than to promise something that you don't follow through on. In such cases, your mouth is making you sin. And don't defend yourself by telling the Temple messenger that the promise you made was a mistake. That would make God angry, and he might wipe out everything you have achieved." When one places his/her hand on The Holy Bible, and takes an oath of office or to give witness to what is true - Integrity in Speech and a Factual representation should be the minimum expectation.

What is expected from others should also be the behavior of us all. In I Corinthians 1:19-20 (NLT), we read: "As the

A Man's Word is His Bond (Or Is It?)

Scriptures say, I will destroy human wisdom and discard their most brilliant ideas. So where does this leave the philosophers, the scholars, and the world's brilliant debaters? God has made them all look foolish and has shown their wisdom to be useless nonsense." Jesus said in Matthew 5:37 (NLT): "Just say a simple, 'Yes, I will,' or 'No, I won't.' Your word is enough. To strengthen your promise with a vow shows that something is wrong." Can anyone - - everyone - - rely on your word? If not, why not?

It would be good if in the ebb and flow of human discourse there was the ability to conceptualize – What's Good for The Goose and Is Good for The Gander. This is one of the idioms we have in the English Language. At the very least, it has a possible gender meaning- such as: What's good for the Male (Gander) should be equally good for the Female (Goose). It is most often used as an explanation for retribution or retaliation – such as, when someone gets back at someone else, makes things even, the justification being if it was good for you to do it to me (or for someone to do it to someone else), it's good for me to do it to you (or for that someone else to do it back to that someone).

Another pesky idiom is "Tit for Tat." An explanation of "Tit for Tat" in Wikipedia is very interesting. "Tit for Tat is an English saying meaning 'equivalent retaliation'. It is also a highly effective strategy in game theory for the iterated prisoner's dilemma. It was first introduced by Anatol Rapoport in Robert Axelrod's two tournaments, held around 1980. An agent using this strategy will initially cooperate, then respond in kind to an opponent's previous action. If the opponent previously was cooperative, the agent is cooperative. If not, the agent is not. This strategy is dependent on four conditions that have allowed it to become the most prevalent strategy for the prisoner's dilemma:

(1) Unless provoked, the agent will always cooperate;
(2) If provoked, the agent will retaliate;
(3) The agent is quick to forgive;

(4) The agent must have a good chance of competing against the opponent more than once.

In the last condition, the definition of 'good chance' depends on the payoff matrix of the prisoner's dilemma. The important thing is that the competition continues long enough for repeated punishment and forgiveness to generate a long-term payoff higher than the possible loss from cooperating initially."

With the above idiom explanations, there is an application to the current Health Care Proposals, Debate, and Enactment. The idea is – if the Health Care Legislation is so good and necessary for the citizenry, why is it not good for the Congress of the United States, and the President, and Labor Unions? Why do they have a choice when the remainder of the citizenry is not afforded the same choice? Why is it that Presidential and Congressional determination is mandated upon the populace that is indicating they do not want this change and Health Care requirement? Why is it that those who will legislate and enact ignore the latest WSJ-NBC News poll regarding President Obama's Health Care initiative where it is indicated and demonstrated that only 36 percent of all poll participants thought the plan was a good idea at this time? Why is it that they disregard Poll Participants who sent an unambiguous message to Congress - only 17 percent approved of the job lawmakers on Capitol Hill are currently doing, and 50 percent of all respondents said that, given the option, they would vote out every member of Congress, including their own representative? How did the nation arrive at such a blatant disconnect?

One other idiom (cliché) is: "Look Before You Leap." The basic idea is to "think carefully about what you are about to do before you do it." Most of us were reared with a constant reminder regarding The Golden Rule, namely, "Do unto others as you would have them do unto you." This should be something deemed very serious and of great importance. After all, in The Sermon on the Mount, Jesus reminded his followers (Matthew 7:12) "So in everything, do to others what you would have them do to you, for this sums up the Law and the Prophets." An underlying moral mandate is given in Leviticus 19:18, "Do not seek revenge or bear a grudge against one of your people, but love your neighbor as yourself. I am the Lord." The summary of Christian focus is given by Jesus Christ in Luke 10:25-28, "…an expert in the law stood up to test Jesus. Teacher…what must I do to inherit eternal life? What is written in the Law? Jesus replied. How do you read it? He answered: Love the Lord your God with all your heart and with all your soul and with all your strength and with all your mind; and, Love your neighbor as yourself. You have answered correctly, Jesus replied. Do this and you will live." No one can improve on that guideline, instruction and mandate. The Congress could argue that this justifies enactment of Universal Health Care. Well, then, why don't they use it themselves before they mandate that everyone else must use it except them?

  A helpful devotional from Day By Day written by Charles R. Swindoll is entitled: "Nostalgic Musings". He writes: "I strolled down Nostalgia Lane with a September 4, 1939, copy of Time Magazine. What a journey! Pickups sold for $465 and best-selling books cost $2. Big news in the music world was Bing Crosby, whose records sold for 35 cents…What was most intriguing, however, was the international scene, as presented by the staff writers. The threat of war was a slumbering giant, and Adolf Hitler's name appeared on almost every page of the Foreign News section. President Franklin Roosevelt was busy calming the troubled waters of our nation's fear of war, speaking openly of his lovely hope for peace. In spite of the Nazi war machine that had already consumed Italy, Sicily, Albania, and was primed to pounce on Poland, Hungary, Belgium, and France, the talk in America was amazingly casual - a smug, business-as-usual attitude. How naive we were! Who knows? Fifty years from now we could be leafing through a Time Magazine yellow with age, feeling a nostalgic twinge and smiling at what we consider modern times. We will no doubt notice the business-as-usual look on our faces, only to be seized with the realization that we had no idea what a ragged edge we were living on in our relaxed American culture. If indeed there is an America fifty years from now. We need to be alert. Sometimes the best of times may be a breeding ground for the worst of times."

In the ongoing focus and reaction to Healthcare Legislation, without missing a beat, THE HILL reports: "Rep. Lynn Woolsey (D-California), the co-chairwoman of the Congressional Progressive Caucus, said she plans to unveil legislation to add the government-run option to the national healthcare exchange established by legislation President Barack Obama is to sign…We will introduce a robust public option bill on the very day the president signs the reconciliation bill into law, Woolsey said Monday during an interview on MSNBC. The public insurance option had been a part of the healthcare legislation first approved by the House in November, but Senate Democratic leaders were forced to abandon the provision after it became clear that they wouldn't be able to get all 60 Democrats to sign onto legislation containing that provision…"

In Day By Day, Charles Swindoll continues: "…it is easy to forget the prophet's warning to beware of those who superficially heal the brokenness of a nation by announcing "peace, peace" when "there is no peace" (Jeremiah 6:14; 8:11). And if we feel sufficiently comfortable and relaxed, it's mighty easy to block from our minds the Savior's prediction of wars and rumors of wars and His warning that "many false prophets will arise and mislead many" (Matthew 24:6-7, 11). The "Me Generation" has won a battle that pleases and satisfies them for now – but – what about down the road – increased taxes; closure of businesses; fines imposed by the IRS for failure to buy Health Insurance, etc.? The Christian who abides in Jesus Christ will retain his/her peace! Jesus Christ assures His followers (John 16:33), "I have told you all this so that you may have peace in me. Here on earth you will have many trials and sorrows. But take heart, because I have overcome the world." It would be wise to turn to Him!

A Man's Word is His Bond (Or Is It?)

In country Gospel Music, Johnny Cash and The Statler Brothers popularize the song: The Fourth Man In The Fire. Some of the lyrics are:

> Now the prophet Daniel tells about
> Three men who walked with God
> Shadrach, Meshach and Abednego
> Before the wicked king they stood
> And the king commanded them bound and thrown
> Into the fiery furnace that day
> But the fire was so hot that the men were slain
> That forced them on their way.
>
> There's Shadrach, Meshach and Abednego
> And the fiery coals they trod
> But the form of the Fourth Man that I see
> Is like the Son of God
> Refrain:
> They wouldn't bend
> They held on to the will of God so we are told
> They wouldn't bow
> They would not bow their knees to Idols made of gold
> They wouldn't burn
> They were protected by the Fourth Man in the fire
> They wouldn't bend
> They wouldn't bow, they wouldn't burn.

The point is – Obey God! Obey His Word! Do what He has Said! It's the only way you can walk in His Victory.

CONSIDER THESE THINGS WITH ME!

Applauding a Train Wreck

Political Pendulums are fascinating to observe! Why? Most of the time they have little, if any, connection to reality. The concern of too many professional politicians is, "what can I do to increase the voter base in order to retain my office and job"! While the Politicians (entirely Democrats) were shown displaying merriment and applauding vigorously their "victory for the people" with the passage of the Health Reform Legislation, The New York Times headlined the following: "Social Security to See Payout Exceed Pay-In This Year" by Mary Williams Walsh, March 24, 2010. In the mad dash for Health Care Reform, the reality of Social Security has received little or no attention by the Professional Politicians. They are too busy applauding their newest Train Wreck in the making. What is the explanation for this Social Security reality?

The article states: "The bursting of the real estate bubble and the ensuing recession have hurt jobs, home prices and now Social Security. This year, the system will pay out more in benefits than it receives in payroll taxes, an important threshold it was not expected to cross until at least 2016, according to the Congressional Budget Office. Stephen C. Goss, chief actuary of the Social Security Administration, said that while the Congressional projection would probably be borne out, the change would have no effect on benefits in 2010 and retirees would keep receiving their checks as usual. The problem, he said, is that payments have risen more than expected during the downturn, because jobs disappeared and people applied for benefits sooner than they had planned. At the same time, the program's revenue has fallen sharply, because there are fewer paychecks to tax. Analysts have long tried to predict the year when Social Security would pay out more than it took in because they view it as a tipping point — the first step of a long, slow march to insolvency, unless Congress strengthens the program's finances. Interestingly, the calculation includes that the Social Security Trust Fund won't reach zero until the year 2037. The Problem is – the trust fund only has government IOUs in it – the money has been spent on other things. Other realities that are seemingly ignored include the passage of Medicare in 1966 with a cost projection of $9 Billion by the year 1990 - the projection was incorrect inasmuch as it exceeded $110 Billion in that time frame. In order to arrive at a projected "savings" for the new Health Care Reform, it includes a reduction in Medicare funding in the amount of $500 billion. Supposedly, this money will be found by ending fraud and abuse in the system! Someone has suggested 12 possible scenarios (guesses) of where Health Care Reform will bring us: (1) Cost overruns; (2) Fraud; (3) Additional coverage extended to groups; (4) Rising deficits in the program; (5) Lower payments to physicians; (6) Lower payments to hospitals; (7) Delays in payments; (8) Rising taxes on the rich; (9) Rationing by doctors, hospitals, government; (10) Delays in treatment; (11) More HMO care, assembly line medicine(12) A search for scapegoats." Regrettably, many of those "guesses" are already realities (Check the Medicaid funding and reimbursement in most States).

    One of the primary issues rests with having Correct Cost Calculations before embarking on a course and in a direction where there are too many variables. When Jesus Christ was challenging people to become a disciple, He told them they should make a Correct Cost Calculation. In Luke 14:28-30, we read: "Suppose one of you wants to build a tower. Will he not first sit down and estimate the cost to see if he has enough money to complete it? For if he lays the foundation and is not able to finish it, everyone who sees it will ridicule him, saying, This fellow began to build and was not able to finish." In this context, the cost includes identity with the Cross, and one's taking it up daily, and then following Jesus Christ. The Message Translations words it: "If you only get the foundation laid and then run out of money, you're going to look pretty foolish. Everyone passing by will poke fun at you: He started something he couldn't finish…"

Applauding a Train Wreck

How long will it take for Health Care Reform to exceed estimates and catch up to the insolvency of Medicare and Social Security? Will those who applauded its passage be there when it fails? Who will Applaud that sure to happen Train Wreck? More importantly, how does one follow Jesus Christ? Have you Correctly Calculated the Cost of following Him? What about the cost of not following Him?

Another part of Applauding A Train Wreck is the absence of civility with many inter-personal relationships, as well as the meltdown in civil and public discourse. On November 7, 2010 Parade Magazine contained an article: "Mr. Smith Flees Washington..." The sub-head was: "Michigan Democrat Bart Stupak got fed up with the mean-spiritedness of D.C. The elections are over. Bart Stupak did not run. After nine terms in Congress, the Democratic representative from Michigan's 1st District is walking away to the winter of his discontent, sadly wondering what happened to the public service he entered 18 years ago…It's so hateful now…Every boundary of decency has been crossed…When did we become so nasty…Stupak sighs. Remember Mr. Smith Goes to Washington? Those days are gone…Mr. Smith no longer dreams of going to Washington. He dreams of leaving it. That cannot be good for America. The irony is that at the end of the Frank Capra movie, Mr. Smith, the senator played by Jimmy Stewart, becomes a shining example of the difference one man can make. Can we become real-life Mr. Smiths and change the ugly tone of our national conversation?"

To the professing Christian and the practicing Church, the Apostle Paul wrote these words in Ephesians 4:29-32, "Let no corrupting talk come out of your mouths, but only such as is good for building up, as fits the occasion, that it may give grace to those who hear. And do not grieve the Holy Spirit of God, by whom you were sealed for the day of redemption. Let all bitterness and wrath and anger and clamor and slander be put away from you, along with all malice. Be kind to one another, tenderhearted, forgiving one another, as God in Christ forgave you." In other words, let civility emanate from you always.

The NLT expresses it this way: "Don't use foul or abusive language. Let everything you say be good and helpful, so that your words will be an encouragement to those who hear them. And do not bring sorrow to God's Holy Spirit by the way you live. Remember, he is the one who has identified you as his own, guaranteeing that you will be saved on the day of redemption. Get rid of all bitterness, rage, anger, harsh words, and slander, as well as all types of malicious behavior. Instead, be kind to each other, tenderhearted, forgiving one another, just as God through Christ has forgiven you." This level behavior is not possible for the secular-minded person who has either avoided or seen no need for a personal relationship with Jesus Christ. If one has ignored the role of the Holy Spirit in ones life, there would be no sensitivity whether or not one was grieving the one who is being ignored.

A problem is that the carnal-type behavior exists among the professing Christian and the practicing Church. It has become a ritual to include as part of a Worship Service – The Lord's Prayer – but to ignore what Jesus stated immediately after teaching His Disciples how to pray. The Prayer includes these words – Matthew 6:12 (NLT) – "and forgive us our sins, just as we have forgiven those who have sinned against us." One can (and does) pray these words each week – but – many refuse to practice it. They would rather hold onto their grudges and biases and mean-spiritedness – anything and everything except obedience to Jesus Christ. What are the words of Jesus that immediately follow this model prayer? How much attention are they given? How willing are you – are we – to implement them and do them – immediately? Okay! Here are the words of Jesus to you – Matthew 6:14-15 (NLT) – "If you forgive those who sin against you, your heavenly Father will forgive you. But if you refuse to forgive others, your Father will not forgive your sins." It cannot be more plain or clear – but still – it is consistently ignored! Why? Do you not believe Jesus Christ said what he meant and means what He has said?

Could it be that you "…bring sorrow to God's Holy Spirit by the way you live…"? If so, you can and should correct this immediately. Reach out to the person(s) you've ignored and/or avoided for years. Be the one who offers the hand of friendship and the words of forgiveness. Be aware that it has to be unconditional and might be received suspiciously as you make the genuine approach and utter the words that can bring healing in a relationship. The words do not need to be extensive or complicated.

Here's the difficult part. You need to be willing to say: "I have said and thought some things about you that are wrong and sinful in God's sight. Please forgive me for that! I truly regret every word and thought that was negative about you. Can we agree to begin to renew our friendship and restore the oneness in Christ that we should have?"

Regardless of how the other person responds or what the other person says, you need to remain sincere and contrite as you humbly reach out in obedience to Jesus Christ.

The adage that allows – "if at first you don't succeed, try, try again" – needs to be the commitment for this approach and effort toward others.

One last thought – if you fail to do this – you are disobeying Jesus Christ and grieving the Holy Spirit of God. The Eternal God is serious about this – and – we should be also.

Please try for Jesus' sake. As you do, you will be the recipient of the fullness of His joy, and the abundance of His peace.

CONSIDER THESE THINGS WITH ME

Phlegmatic Philosophy

Two areas that can generate much debate are Politics and Religion. When Politics intrudes into Religion, the friction it causes usually generates more heat than light. The scope and sincerity of the speaker, as well as what is spoken will be scrutinized. Great care should be exercised so that one's belief system doesn't alienate a nation founded upon certain values and traditions. If the speaker is somewhat phlegmatic in his approach, more harm than good will ensue from what is being spoken. Consider the Thesaurus presentation for phlegmatic: as an adjective it means unemotional. Some of the primary Synonyms are: cool, apathetic, disinterested, dispassionate, unexcitable, unfeeling, uninvolved...

There is usually a Presidential Proclamation issued at Easter that is focused on the traditional values of that seasonal observance in the Judeo-Christian beliefs and practices. In his April 3rd, 2010 Weekly Address, President Obama stated: "This is a week of faithful celebration. On Monday and Tuesday nights, Jewish families and friends in the United States and around the world gathered for a Seder to commemorate the Exodus from Egypt and the triumph of hope and perseverance over injustice and oppression. On Sunday, my family will join other Christians all over the world in marking the resurrection of Jesus Christ. And while we worship in different ways, we also remember the shared spirit of humanity that inhabits us all – Jews and Christians, Muslims and Hindus, believers and nonbelievers alike...These are aspirations that stretch back through the ages – aspirations at the heart of Judaism, at the heart of Christianity, at the heart of all of the world's great religions. The rites of Passover, and the traditions of Easter, have been marked by people in every corner of the planet for thousands of years. They have been marked in times of peace, in times of upheaval, in times of war...Their only hope that this unity will endure...Happy Easter and Happy Passover to all those celebrating, here in America, and around the world."

By comparison, the 2008 Easter Proclamation issued by George W. Bush, President of the United States...stated: "I am the resurrection and the life. He who believes in me will live, even though he dies." John 11:25 – "Laura and I send greetings to all those celebrating the joyful holiday of Easter. The Resurrection of Jesus Christ reminds people around the world of the presence of a faithful God who offers a love more powerful than death. Easter commemorates our Savior's triumph over sin, and we take joy in spending this special time with family and friends and reflecting on the many blessings that fill our lives. During this season of renewal, let us come together and give thanks to the Almighty who made us in His image and redeemed us in His love. On this glorious day, we remember our brave men and women in uniform who are separated from their families by great distances. We pray for their safety and strength, and we honor those who gave their lives to advance peace and secure liberty across the globe. Happy Easter. May God bless you, and may God bless our great Nation."

A Christian Nation should have some prerequisites for its Leaders – not the least of which would be a dependence upon the Lord. In II Kings 18:13-19: "The king of Assyria sent his supreme commander, his chief officer and his field commander with a large army...to King Hezekiah...They came up to Jerusalem and stopped at the aqueduct of the Upper Pool...They called for the king; and...the field commander said to them, Tell Hezekiah: This is what the great king, the king of Assyria, says: On what are you basing this confidence of yours?" In II Kings 19:14-19, we see what King Hezekiah did: "(He)...went up to the temple of the Lord and spread the letter out before the Lord. And Hezekiah prayed..."O Lord, God of Israel...Give ear, O Lord, and hear; open your eyes, O Lord, and see; listen to the words Sennacherib has sent to insult the living God...Now, O Lord our God, deliver us from his hand, so that all kingdoms on earth may know that you alone, O Lord, are God." What has happened to our nation? Why is it we have allowed the negatives to dominate the positives? Why is it we have allowed cultural values to supplant Christian values? Why do we allow ourselves to march toward the dangerous precipice of loss, defeat and oblivion? The time to reverse course is now! The time to seek the Lord and His help is long past due!

It seems as though those who have the rule and authority over us view their obligation more as a "game" rather than a duty to safeguard the core values that were foundational to the birth of the nation. As this nation developed, it seldom strayed from its ore values. When it did, convincing voices were raised and a determined citizenry was ready to sacrifice in order that the core values would remain.

In the 18th Century, a movement began that essentially believed there should be "No Taxation Without Representation." The issue pertained to the imposition of taxes by Great Britain upon the 13 Colonies. When the British sent troops to the colonies to enforce the Tax levy, it led to The Revolutionary War and the writing of The Declaration of Independence. Fast-forward to the 21st Century - Are you, as a legal citizen of this country, adequately and properly represented? In a practical sense, is it possible that the nation once again has to endure Taxation Without Representation? Taking this one step further, do you feel that the Congress is spending and incurring debt without any regard for those they have been elected to represent?

Charlie Reese, a former columnist of The Orlando Sentinel Newspaper has written an article entitled: 545 People. He states: "Politicians are the only people in the world who create problems and then campaign against them. Have you ever wondered, if both the Democrats and the Republicans are against deficits, why do we have deficits? Have you ever wondered, if all the politicians are against inflation and high taxes, why do we have inflation and high taxes? You and I don't propose a federal budget. The president does. You and I don't have the Constitutional authority to vote on appropriations. The House of Representatives does. You and I don't write the tax code, Congress does. You and I don't set fiscal policy, Congress does. You and I don't control monetary policy, the Federal Reserve Bank does. One hundred senators, 435 congress-men, one president, and nine Supreme Court Justices equates to 545 human beings out of the 300 million are directly, legally, morally, and individually responsible for the domestic problems that plague this country. I excluded the members of the Federal Reserve Board because that problem was created by the Congress. In 1913, Congress delegated its Constitutional duty to provide a sound currency to a federally chartered, but private, central bank. I excluded all the special interests and lobbyists for a sound reason. They have no legal authority. They have no ability to coerce a senator, a congressman, or a president to do one…thing. I don't care if they offer a politician $1 million dollars in cash. The politician has the power to accept or reject it. No matter what the lobbyist promises, it is the legislator's responsibility to determine how he votes. Those 545 human beings spend much of their energy convincing you that what they did is not their fault. They cooperate in this common con regardless of party."

"What separates a politician from a normal human being is an excessive amount of gall. No normal human being would have the gall of a Speaker, who stood up and criticized the President for creating deficits…The President can only propose a budget. He cannot force the Congress to accept it. The Constitution, which is the supreme law of the land, gives sole responsibility to the House of Representatives for originating and approving appropriations and taxes. It seems inconceivable…that a nation of 300 million can not replace 545 people who stand convicted - by present facts - of incompetence and irresponsibility. I can't think of a single domestic problem that is not traceable directly to those 545 people. When you fully grasp the plain truth that 545 people exercise the power of the federal government, then it must follow that what exists is what they want to exist. If the tax code is unfair, it's because they want it unfair. If the budget is in the red, it's because they want it in the red...If the Army and Marines are in Iraq, it's because they want them in Iraq. If they do not receive social security but are on an elite retirement plan not available to the people, it's because they want it that way..."

When the Lord issues His assessment of the nation and people in Jeremiah 5:30-31 (NLT), He says: "A horrible and shocking thing has happened in this land - the Prophets give false prophecies, and the Priests rule with an iron hand. And worse yet, my people like it that way! But what will you do when the end comes?" This nation is nearing the abyss of uncertainty, demise and/or destruction. Warnings are met with ridicule! Those who govern are dismissive of those they supposedly represent. Apparently, the people love to have it that way because they keep electing the same people to office – year after year! We can do better! While you have the opportunity you should insist on it!

CONSIDER THESE THINGS WITH ME!

Hyphenated-Fixation

Recent generations have become more aware of the use of Hyphens to define and designate various ethnic and people groups, as well as organizations and what the purportedly represent. It can be thought of as a Hyphen-Fixation or a Hyphen-Hypertension. We have also become aware and accustomed to the use of Acronyms. In some ways, Hyphens are more easily understood than Acronyms. Consider some well-known Acronyms: "AIDS: acquired immune deficiency syndrome; SCUBA: self-contained underwater breathing apparatus; RADAR: radio detection and ranging; AAA: American Automobile Association, or Abdominal Aortic Aneurysm, or Anti-Aircraft Artillery, or Amateur Athletic Association; ATM: automated teller machine; PIN: personal identification number; UPC: Universal Product Code. Probably the most notorious Acronym recently publicized has been A.C.O.R.N.: The Association of Community Organizations for Reform Now,

The use of Hyphens is also common-place. An example is: "Census Bureau Counting Same-Sex Couples." The following observation is made by way of commentary: "In the first U.S. census that will tally same-sex couples who say they are married — even those without a marriage license — gay-rights activists are urging maximum participation by their community with the strong backing from the Census Bureau. Only the District of Columbia and five states — Massachusetts, Connecticut, New Hampshire, Vermont and Iowa — have legalized gay marriages. But, the Census Bureau says same-sex couples in any state who consider themselves "spouses" should feel free to check the "husband" or "wife" boxes on the census form, rather than "unmarried partner." Tony Perkins, president of the Family Research Council, says the Defense of Marriage Act forbids the federal government from recognizing same-sex relationships as "marriages." "The President's Commerce Department is actively encouraging people to ignore U.S. marriage law and invent new definitions for their relationships," Perkins said. "What kind of government actively lobbies citizens to lie on their forms?" [The Associated Press, CitizenLink.com]

If one has responsibly taken the time to open and fill in the Census 2010 form, the Hyphenated Factor is very predictable. Question 8: Is Person 1 of Hispanic, Latino, or Spanish origin? In Question 9: What is Person 1's Race? And then the list of selections: White; Black; African American, or Negro; American Indian or Alaskan Native. The list continues with Asian Indian, Chinese, Filipino, Japanese, Korean, Vietnamese, Native Hawaiian, Guamanian or Chamorro, Samoan, or Other Pacific Islander. In some regard, it is easy to understand why the designations are solicited, but one can only suppose that the emerging or dominant groups will become a Hyphenated-Group before long. Why can't we all be just American without hyphens?

There are several names of God, especially in the Old Testament, that are Hyphenated. They express different aspects of the Lord's care and relationship with His people. They communicate a great truth – God is totally adequate! Some examples are:

> JEHOVAH-ROHI - Psalm 23:1
> "The Lord my shepherd"
> JEHOVAH-SHAMMAH - Ezekiel 48:35
> "The Lord who is present"
> JEHOVAH-RAPHA - Exodus 15:26
> "The Lord our healer"
> JEHOVAH-TSIDKENU - Jeremiah 23:6
> "The Lord our righteousness"
> JEHOVAH-JIREH - Genesis 22:13-14
> "The Lord will provide"
> JEHOVAH-NISSI - Exodus 17:15
> "The Lord our banner"
> JEHOVAH-SHALOM - Judges 6:24
> "The Lord is peace"

Hyphenated-Fixation

JEHOVAH-SABBAOTH - Isaiah 6:1-3
"The Lord of Hosts"
EL-ELYON - Genesis 14:17-20, Isaiah 14:13-14
"The Most High God
EL-SHADDAI - Genesis 17:1, Psalm 91:1
"The Almighty God"

God wants to be known in a personal and intimate way. He wants to be known as The One Who is more than sufficient at all times and for all things for those who trust in Him. Paul gives some summary to this in Ephesians 3:20-12, "Now to him who is able to do immeasurably more than all we ask or imagine, according to his power that is at work within us, to him be glory in the church and in Christ Jesus throughout all generations, for ever and ever! Amen. This God (hyphens and all) can be known personally by you. The problem is never with God – it is always man and how he understands and replies to God.

There are all too many people who could be described as Witless and Wistful Wimps. They exhibit a Will-O'-The-Wisp ("anything that deludes or misleads by luring on") characteristic. The Encyclopedia Britannica indicates that: "in meteorology, a Will-O'-The-Wisp is a mysterious light seen at night flickering over marshes; when approached, it advances, always out of reach." In some ways, it is similar to The Cowardly Lion in The Wizard of Oz who silently lives with his fears due to his sense of inadequacy and perceived lack of Courage. He doesn't seem to understand that Courage means acting in spite of and in the face of Fear.

On April 27, 2009 an article appeared in the Russian Pravda News Site. It is entitled "American Capitalism Gone With A Whimper", written by Stanislav Mishin. Some of the shared thoughts are: "It must be said, that like the breaking of a great dam, the American descent into Marxism is happening with breath-taking speed, against the back drop of a passive, hapless sheeple, excuse me dear reader, I meant people…The initial testing grounds was conducted upon our Holy Russia and a bloody test it was. But we Russians would not just roll over and give up our freedoms and our souls, no matter how much money Wall Street poured into the fists of the Marxists. Those lessons were taken and used to properly prepare the American populace for the surrender of their freedoms and souls, to the whims of their elites and betters. First, the population was dumbed-down through a politicized and substandard education system based on pop culture, rather than the classics. Second, their faith in God was destroyed, until their churches, all tens of thousands of different branches and denominations were for the most part little more than Sunday circuses and their televangelists and top protestant mega preachers were more than happy to sell out their souls and flocks to be on the winning side of one pseudo Marxist politician or another. Third, the final collapse has come with the election of Barack Obama. His speed…has been truly impressive. His spending and money printing has been a record setting, not just in America's short history but in the world. If this keeps up for more than another year, and there is no sign that it will not, America at best will resemble the Weimar Republic and at worst Zimbabwe… There came the announcement of a planned redesign of the American Byzantine tax system, by the very thieves who used it to bankroll their thefts, losses, and swindles of hundreds of billions of dollars. These make our Russian oligarchs look little more than ordinary street thugs, in comparison. Yes, the Americans have beat our own thieves in the shear volumes. Should we congratulate them? These men, of course, are not an elected panel but made up of appointees picked from the very financial oligarchs and their henchmen who are now gorging themselves on trillions of American dollars, in one bailout after another. They are also usurping the rights, duties, and powers of the American congress (parliament). Again, congress has put up little more than a whimper to their masters…Apparently, even though we suffered 70 years of this Western sponsored horror show, we know nothing, as foolish, drunken Russians, so let our

"wise" Anglo-Saxon fools find out the folly of their own pride. Again, the American public has taken this with barely a whimper...but a 'free man' whimper." See:
http://www.snopes.com/politics/soapbox/pravda.asp

    Obviously, those who stand for nothing will fall for anything! An Earth Worm has more spine than many of our citizens. Too many are focused on what they deem to be their vested interests than they are to stand on principle and for what is right. They are willing to accept the inevitable without so much as a whimper. An illustration of this is in I Kings 18:21 when Elijah is in the Contest with The Prophets of Baal. "Elijah went before the people and said, How long will you waver between two opinions? If the Lord is God, follow him; but if Baal is God, follow him. But the people said nothing." Not a whimper! No demonstrated commitment! No willingness to be involved! No standing on principle! No courage in a vital cause! Just witless and/or wistful! No whimper or word of support for Elijah.

    More than 50 years ago, Paul Tillich wrote a tome with an intriguing title: The Courage To Be. He notes: "The break-down of absolutism…" and observes: "In this the anxiety of emptiness and meaninglessness is dominant. We are under the threat of spiritual non-being." That's what Witless and Wistful Non-Whimpering Wimps embrace.

    There needs to be courageous men and women who will stand in the gap with courage, principle, commitment and fortitude. For those who are either wistful or wimpish, God's Grace is sufficient – and – His strength will be perfected in your weakness. Trust Him and Prove Him!

CONSIDER THESE THINGS WITH ME!

What is Truth? - What is Fiction?

What is Fact? What is Fiction? What is True? What is False? Has Fantasy, Fraud, and Fiction supplanted Fact, Truth, and Reliability? Does it matter any more? Truth and Integrity seem to have been sacrificed; fiction has been substituted for reality; and journalism has yielded to "something feigned, invented, or imagined."

In the earthly ministry of the Lord Jesus Christ, a question was posed to him – John 14:4-6 – "And you know the way to where I am going. Thomas said to him, Lord, we do not know where you are going. How can we know the way? Jesus said to him, I am the way, and the truth, and the life. No one comes to the Father except through me." Thomas received a more detailed response to his question: How can we know the way?" The broadened answer is by knowing The One Who is not only the way – but also – the truth and the life. Someone once paraphrased that verse to read: I am the way and the life – that's the absolute truth.

This issue of truth would arise once more in the life and ministry of Jesus Christ. Jesus is on trial before Pilate. In John 18:37-38, the subject of Truth arises: "Then Pilate said to him, So you are a king? Jesus answered, You say that I am a king. For this purpose I was born and for this purpose I have come into the world--to bear witness to the truth. Everyone who is of the truth listens to my voice. Pilate said to him, What is truth? After he had said this, he went back outside to the Jews and told them, I find no guilt in him." The critical and prevailing question posed by Pilate: What Is Truth? Is the world and culture ready to acknowledge and receive Jesus Christ Who declared Himself to be The Truth?

In our secular society and culture, the level of trust and believability has waned. This is borne out by an Associated Press Headline article By Liz Sidoti reads: "Poll: 4 Out Of 5 Americans

Don't Trust Washington." It's not just isolated to Washington. It is pandemic throughout all areas of the nation and life. She writes: "America's Great Compromiser, Henry Clay, called government the great trust, but most Americans today have little faith in Washington's ability to deal with the nation's problems. Public confidence in government is at one of the lowest points in a half century, according to a survey from the Pew Research Center. Nearly 8 in 10 Americans say they don't trust the federal government and have little faith it can solve America's ills, the survey found."

Peggy Noonan is a very gifted and creative writer. In The Wall Street Journal: April 9, 2010, she wrote: "After the Crash, A Crashing Bore." In her desire to see some indication of Transparency in the climate of our times, she resorted to both Fiction and Hyperbole (an extravagant statement or figure of speech not intended to be taken literally) to make an important point: "The men behind the bailout take refuge in impenetrable jargon. Like all Americans, I continue to seek to understand exactly what moods, facts, assumptions, dynamics, agendas and structures underlay and made possible the crash and the Great Recession... That's why the Financial Industry Inquiry Commission hearings were so exciting, such a public service. The testimony of Charles Prince, former CEO of Citigroup, a too-big-to-fail bank that received $45 billion in bailouts and $300 billion in taxpayer guarantees, was riveting. You've seen it on the news, but if you were watching it live on C-Span, the stark power of his brutal candor was breathtaking. This, as you know, is what he said: Let's be real. This is what happened the past 10 years. You, for political reasons, both Republicans and Democrats, finagled the mortgage system so that people who make, like, zero dollars a year were given mortgages for $600,000 houses. You got to run around and crow about how under your watch everyone became a homeowner.

You shook down the taxpayer and hoped for the best. Democrats did it because they thought it would make everyone

What is Truth? - What is Fiction?

Democrats: Look what I give you! Republicans did it because they thought it would make everyone Republicans: I'm a homeowner, I've got a stake, don't raise my property taxes, get off my lawn!' And Wall Street? We bundled the mortgages and sold them to fools, or we held them, called them assets, and made believe everyone would pay their mortgage. As if we cared. We invented financial instruments so complicated no one, even the people who sold them, understood what they were. You're finaglers and we're finaglers. I play for dollars, you play for votes. In our own ways we're all thieves. We would be called desperadoes if we weren't so boring, so utterly banal in our soft-jawed, full-jowled selfishness. If there were any justice, we'd be forced to duel, with the peasants of America holding our cloaks. Only we'd both make sure we missed, wouldn't we?"

Noonan continues: "OK, Charles Prince didn't say that - he would never say something so dramatic and intemperate. I made it up. It wasn't on the news because it didn't happen. It would be kind of a breath of fresh air though, wouldn't it?" Then - the News on April 16, 2010: "The government accused Wall Street's most powerful firm of fraud, saying Goldman Sachs & Co. sold mortgage investments without telling the buyers that the securities were crafted with input from a client who was betting on them to fail. And fail they did. The securities cost investors close to $1 billion while helping Goldman client Paulson & Co., a hedge fund, capitalize on the housing bust. The Goldman executive accused of shepherding the deal allegedly boasted about the exotic trades he created without necessarily understanding all of the implications of those monstrosities!!!" What separates Truth from Fiction? A Biblical Guideline that should be embraced and adhered to is: II Corinthians 8:20-21, "We want to avoid any criticism…For we are taking pains to do what is right, not only in the eyes of the Lord but also in the eyes of men." And, Romans 12:17, "Be careful to do what is right in the eyes of everybody." To walk in Truth and Integrity is a life-choice and a life-style. It has been called – "Spiritual Breathing!" We need to do it!

In the ebb and flow of economic upheaval, some were clamoring for investigations to delve into the Bare Facts and Naked Truths of what has been occurring in both the major banks and businesses in this nation, as well as in behind the scenes Government pandering and promised financial relief.

How should crises be handled? Who is responsible to initiate some action of oversight? What did Nero allegedly do while Rome was burning? What does an American President do while Washington, DC is faltering and in turmoil? What do the minions in Government do when oversight is their task? Do they fiddle? Do they play another round of Golf? Or – is there some other diversion to keep one from focusing on the immediate and to defer his thought processes and energies in other directions?

In a Byline of the Daily News on April 23, 2010 Leo Standora wrote: "While Economy Crumbled, Top Financial Watchdogs at SEC Surfed for Porn on Internet." In particular, what were the Senior Staffers at the Security and Exchange Commission doing while the economy was in a free fall? Standora continues: "The country's top financial watchdogs…spent hours gawking at porn Web sites as the economy teetered on the brink, according to a memo released Thursday night. The shocking findings include Securities and Exchange Commission senior staffers using government computers to browse…and an accountant who tried to access the raunchy sites 16,000 times in one month. Their…pastime was discovered during 33 probes of employees looking at explicit images in the past five years, said the memo obtained by The Associated Press. Among the startling findings: (1) A senior attorney at the SEC's Washington headquarters spent up to eight hours a day looking at and downloading pornography. When his government computer ran out of hard drive space, he burned the files to CDs or DVDs. He later agreed to resign. (2) An accountant was blocked more than 16,000 times in a single month from visiting…pornography" sites, but still managed to amass a collection of very graphic material by using Google to bypass the SEC's internal filter. He wound up with a 2-

week suspension. (3) Seventeen of the employees were at a senior level earning salaries of up to $222,418…" The Washington Post contained the same information received from the Associated Press.

A similar report in the Washington Times from 2009 indicated: "Porn Surfing Rampant at U.S. Science Foundation…Number of Cases Overwhelms Watchdog, Costs Taxpayers" By Jim McElhatton. "Employee misconduct investigations, often involving workers accessing pornography from their government computers, grew six-fold last year…" Is this acceptable behavior? Does this reflect the moral standards you maintain and desire Government officials to embrace? Is this evidence of compromise run amuck? Do you care? Does anyone really care?

"The problems at the National Science Foundation (NSF) were so pervasive they swamped the agency's Inspector General and forced the internal watchdog to cut back on its primary mission of investigating grant fraud and recovering misspent tax dollars. To manage this dramatic increase without an increase in staff required us to significantly reduce our efforts to investigate grant fraud, the Inspector General recently told Congress in a budget request. We anticipate a significant decline in investigative recoveries and prosecutions in coming years as a direct result…One senior executive spent at least 331 days looking at pornography on his government computer and chatting online with nude or partially clad women…the records show. When finally caught, the NSF official retired. He even offered, among other explanations, a humanitarian defense, suggesting that he frequented the porn sites to provide a living to the poor overseas women…He explained that these young women are from poor countries and need to make money to help their parents and this site helps them do that," investigators wrote in a memo.

Lamont Cranston was a crime-fighting vigilante with psychic powers who appeared as The Shadow in a 1930s radio drama. The program began with a question: "Who Knows What

Evil Lurks In The Hearts of Men…?" With a crackling voice, he would respond: "The Shadow Knows….!" It is more important to know and realize that Almighty God knows. In Matthew 15:16-18, Jesus was explaining a parable to His Disciples and stated:" the things that come out of the mouth come from the heart, and these make a man unclean. For out of the heart come evil thoughts, murder, adultery, sexual immorality, theft, false testimony, slander. These are what make a man unclean." The instruction in Proverbs 4:23-27 should be heeded: "Guard your heart above all else, for it determines the course of your life. Avoid all perverse talk; stay away from corrupt speech. Look straight ahead, and fix your eyes on what lies before you. Mark out a straight path for your feet; stay on the safe path. Don't get sidetracked; keep your feet from following evil."

There is a section in John Bunyan's "The Pilgrim's Progress" where Christian and Hopeful approach the Delectable Mountains near the Celestial City. They encounter wise shepherds who warn them of the treacherous mountains Error and Caution, where previous pilgrims have died. The shepherds point out travelers who wander among tombs nearby, having been blinded by the Giant Despair. They warn the travelers to beware of shortcuts, which may be paths to hell. The two pilgrims meet Ignorance, a sprightly teenager who believes that living a good life is sufficient to prove one's religious faith. Christian refutes him, and Ignorance decides to avoid their company. The travelers also meet Flatterer, who snares them in a net, and Atheist, who denies that the Celestial City exists. Crossing the sleep-inducing Enchanted Ground, they try to stay awake by discussing Hopeful's sinful past and religious doctrine. Christian and Hopeful gleefully approach the land of Beulah, where the Celestial City is located. The landscape teems with flowers and fruit, and the travelers are refreshed. To reach the gate into the city, they must first cross a river without a bridge. Christian nearly drowns, but Hopeful reminds him of Christ's love, and Christian emerges safely from the water. The residents of the Celestial City joyously welcome the two pilgrims.

In this journey by Pilgrim, he encountered many naysayers, all kinds of discouragements, and all sorts of spurious and negative counsel/advice. His choice was clear and precise – keep your eye on the Wicket Gate to the Celestial City. We, like Pilgrim come across many discouragements, negative advice and distractions. We, like Pilgrim, have a clear and precise choice. In our case, it is not to look at or lust for a mere gate. Our direction is different. We read it in Hebrews 12:1-3 (NKJV), "we also, since we are surrounded by so great a cloud of witnesses, let us lay aside every weight, and the sin which so easily ensnares us, and let us run with endurance the race that is set before us, looking unto Jesus, the author and finisher of our faith, who for the joy that was set before Him endured the cross, despising the shame, and has sat down at the right hand of the throne of God. For consider Him who endured such hostility from sinners against Himself, lest you become weary and discouraged in your souls."

This is your direction and opportunity. Don't ignore it and don't miss it!

CONSIDER THESE THINGS WITH ME!

Should Topsy-Turvy Be Cloned?

Life was far more predictable before someone messed around with Topsy-Turvy! The equilibrium might have been off slightly – but at least we knew we could make heads or tails out of most situations. But then – someone or something got to Topsy-Turvy - (meaning: "with the top downward and the bottom up; upside-down.; in or into a state of utter disorder or confusion). Has anyone seen or tried to clone Topsy-Turvy? We knew that Topsy-Turvy was where most have lived during their lifetime. There was something about it that kept everyone comfortable and not too distressed with most of life-situation experiences that came ones way.

Then a decision was made by someone – an Anti-Topsy-Turvy-Type person – to remove religion from our way of life; to submit to psycho-analysis and psychological behavioral counseling; to take medication for attention disorder; to minimize the work effort and incentive by instituting entitlement programs planned and controlled by the government; etc. – and all-too-quickly – Topsy-Turvy was no longer prominent among us. We had lost a well-known companion and friend. It would be good if Topsy-Turvy would reappear. It was like a death of a close friend – someone who is fading in our memories. Some have offered something similar, as though a clone was possible, but it was easily an abject failure.

Why is there such polarization in our country, Congress and Government today? Why is there such rivalry among the nations of the world? Why is it that the Courts (Judges and Lawyers) cannot agree on Constitutional Law? Why is it that Churches fall into disarray and oftentimes divide? Does the Church believe that being one in the Biblical sense is equivalent to being an island unto oneself? Is it possible that forgetting about and ignoring Topsy-Turvy is The Reason for all the turmoil, conflict and division in institutions, lives of people, and governments of our world?

As odd as it may seem, sometimes marriage can be a cause of the loss of Topsy-Turvy. One spouse is a neat-type person – the other is a leave-it-laying-around type. This writer knows – his spouse comes with her duster and wants the desk set in order and things put away so she can dust. The failure here is that the desk is so covered with "important documentation" there is no room for the dust to accumulate. However, things get rearranged and Topsy-Turvy has lost another haven. Now the chore is to locate the items that were made to be relocated.

It should be easy to understand the response and reaction of King Hezekiah in II Kings 20:1-11, The gist of the historical narrative is: "In those days Hezekiah became ill and was at the point of death. The prophet Isaiah went to him and said, This is what the Lord says: Put your house in order, because you are going to die; you will not recover." In other words, straighten out the Topsy-Turvy stuff in your life! This is check-out time for you!" There's an interesting turn here, namely, Hezekiah wanted to continue living – maybe in part because of all the Topsy-Turvy details he had put off to "some other day"! Note what happens: "Hezekiah turned his face to the wall and prayed to the Lord, Remember, O Lord, how I have walked before you faithfully and with wholehearted devotion and have done what is good in your eyes. And Hezekiah wept bitterly. Before Isaiah had left the middle court, the word of the Lord came to him: Go back and tell Hezekiah, the leader of my people, This is what the Lord, the God of your father David, says: I have heard your prayer and seen your tears; I will heal you. On the third day from now you will go up to the temple of the Lord. I will add fifteen years to your life. And I will deliver you and this city from the hand of the king of Assyria. I will defend this city for my sake and for the sake of my servant David…"

In some ways, Topsy-Turvy is alright. In other ways, it is not! Matthew 5:23-26 enjoins that Topsy-Turvy delays are not acceptable. Note: "First go and be reconciled to your brother; then come and offer your gift. Settle matters quickly with your adversary..." Keep short accounts with each other! Justice Delayed is Justice Denied. The points of emphasis are: (1) First Go, and (2) Settle Matters Quickly. Maybe we need to let Topsy-Turvy be in seclusion for now! Time seems to be running out and we need to do what must be done to set things in order while we have these moments to do it.

Something has happened in and to the culture and average lifestyle that is more critical than a major health issue – we are forgetting how to have Fun. In most areas of life – politics, religion, international matters, and health concerns - we seem to be on a Collision Course. Choose a side in this societal free-for-all! It would be almost a breath of fresh air if someone flamboyant appeared – someone who could cause a cross-section of people to forget about issues that cause division and conflict – and to focus on what might be classified as either the ridiculous, humorous or maybe – subtlety sublime. As we reminisced about Topsy-Turvy, maybe a search for the flamboyant and fragrant might be in order. We could call it The Search For Gorgeous George. Gorgeous George came on the scene following the Great Depression and near the conclusion of World War II. He had no limit to his Flamboyant manner and display. In actually, he was: "George Raymond Wagner (March 1915–December 1963) who became an American professional wrestler best known by his ring name Gorgeous George. In the United States, during the First Golden Age of Professional Wrestling in the 1940s-1950s, Gorgeous George gained mainstream popularity and became one of the biggest stars of this period, gaining media attention for his outrageous character, which was described as flamboyant and charismatic. When Someone or Some Thing is Flamboyant, it is said to be: "strikingly bold or brilliant; showy; conspicuously dashing and colorful..."

That definition described Gorgeous George. He debuted and dramatized his new glamour boy image on a 1941 card in

Eugene, Oregon; and he quickly antagonized the fans with his exaggerated effeminate behavior when the ring announcer introduced him as Gorgeous George. Such showmanship was unheard of for the time; and consequently, arena crowds grew in size as fans turned out to ridicule George…He would be known as the Human Orchid as he throw his kisses and flowers to the chanting crowd. His persona was created in part by growing his hair long, dyeing it platinum blonde, and putting gold-plated bobby pins in it (he called them "Georgie Pins" while distributing them to the audience). Furthermore, he transformed his ring entrance into a bona-fide spectacle that would often take up more time than his actual matches. He was the first wrestler to really use entrance music, as he strolled nobly to the ring to the sounds of "Pomp and Circumstance," followed by his valet and a purple spotlight. Wearing an elegant robe sporting an array of sequins, Gorgeous George was always escorted down a personal red carpet by his ring valet "Jeffries," who would carry a silver mirror while spreading rose petals at his feet. While George removed his robe, Jeffries would spray the ring with disinfectant (Chanel No. 5 perfume), which George referred to as "Chanel #10" ("Why be half-safe?") before he would start wrestling. Moreover, George required that his valets spray the referee's hands before the official was allowed to check him for any illegal objects, which thus prompted his now-famous outcry "Get your filthy hands off me!" Once the match finally began, he would cheat in every way he could. This flamboyant image and his showman's ability to work a crowd to a near frenzy were so successful in the early days of television that he became the most famous wrestler of his time.

      In the Christian religion, there just might be room and a place for someone who is both Flamboyant and capable of spreading that which is Fragrant. Consider what the Apostle Paul was intimating in II Corinthians 2:14-17, "But thanks be to God, who always leads us in triumphal procession in Christ and through us spreads everywhere the fragrance of the knowledge of him. For we are to God the aroma of Christ among those who are being saved and those who are perishing. To the one we are the smell of death; to the other, the fragrance of life. And who is equal to such a task? Unlike so many, we do not peddle the word of God for profit. On the contrary, in Christ we speak before God with sincerity, like men sent from God."

Allow your imagination to think of the impact one could make if Pomp and Circumstance indicated the "Triumphal Procession In Christ", and Chanel No.5 used to indicate "The Fragrance of the Knowledge of Christ." You may immediately recoil at the thought – but – how well do you do at demonstrating the Triumphal Procession in Christ and being the Fragrance of the Knowledge of Him? We need to seek and use creative ways and means as we endeavor to Know Him and Make Him Known!

Why is it that being the fragrance of Christ is so foreign to individual lives and the Church as a whole? How did we arrive at the point where such a reality is so regularly ignored? When and Why did we jettison relationship and commitment to Jesus Christ as the Number One priority for both a Christian Life and the Christian Church?

Every year there is a day designated as Earth Day. The idea is to take care of the Planet, Littering… Pollution… Contamination, etc. People who do not care are all part of our ongoing experience and frustration. What is often missed and/or forgotten is at the Creation of the world, a Cultural Mandate was issued by the Creator – Genesis 1:28 – "And God said to them, Be fruitful and multiply and fill the earth and subdue it and have dominion over the fish of the sea and over the birds of the heavens and over every living thing that moves on the earth." It was a right priority then and it is a right priority now. The idea that everyone should exercise care for the Environment and the Planet is, in actuality, an obvious responsibility for each inhabitant.

However, in the concern for the Planet, there are those who are given to Absurdities, Speculations and Ignorance. The

Alarmists and Speculators in their Earth Day Predictions offered 40 years ago, in 1970, included some of the following:

An Ecologist, Kenneth Watt stated - "We have about five more years at the outside to do something." and "At the present rate of nitrogen buildup, it's only a matter of time before light will be filtered out of the atmosphere and none of our land will be usable." Also, "By the year 2000, if present trends continue, we will be using up crude oil at such a rate...that there won't be any more crude oil. You'll drive up to the pump and say, Fill 'er up, buddy, and he'll say, I am very sorry, there isn't any." – and - "The world has been chilling sharply for about twenty years. If present trends continue, the world will be about four degrees colder for the global mean temperature in 1990, but eleven degrees colder in the year 2000. This is about twice what it would take to put us into an ice age."

A Biologist, Paul Ehrlich stated: "Population will inevitably and completely outstrip whatever small increases in food supplies we make. The death rate will increase until at least 100-200 million people per year will be starving to death during the next ten years." – and - "By...1975, some experts feel that food shortages will have escalated the present level of world hunger and starvation into famines of unbelievable proportions. Other experts, more optimistic, think the ultimate food-population collision will not occur until the decade of the 1980s."

An additional speculation given by Peter Gunter, professor, North Texas State University states: "Demographers agree almost unanimously on the following grim timetable: by 1975 widespread famines will begin in India; these will spread by 1990 to include all of India, Pakistan, China and the Near East, Africa. By the year 2000, or conceivably sooner, South and Central America will exist under famine conditions...By the year 2000, thirty years from now, the entire world, with the exception of Western Europe, North America, and Australia, will be in famine."

Should Topsy-Turvy Be Cloned?

The basic thesis of the Global Warming focus group is that there will be: "An increase in global temperature that will cause sea levels to rise and will change the amount and pattern of precipitation, probably including expansion of subtropical deserts. Warming is expected to be strongest in the Arctic and would be associated with continuing retreat of glaciers, permafrost and sea ice. Other likely effects include changes in the frequency and intensity of extreme weather events, species extinctions, and changes in agricultural yields. Warming and related changes will vary from region to region around the globe, though the nature of these regional variations is uncertain."

Those who offer these statements are undaunted in their speculations and beliefs. Although some are very sincere, they are also sincerely wrong. But Note - a Day of Global Warming and Planetary disruption will occur. In II Peter 3:8-12, we read this description: "the day of the Lord will come like a thief. The heavens will disappear with a roar; the elements will be destroyed by fire, and the earth and everything in it will be laid bare. Since everything will be destroyed in this way, what kind of people ought you to be? That day will bring about the destruction of the heavens by fire, and the elements will melt in the heat." This passage, along with Matthew 24 and 25 are not speculating about "The Day of the Lord."

It is a fact that there will be a day of judgment! It is a fact that there will be a day when the universe as we know it will be altered by the Power of the Lord. It is a fact that the Holy Scriptures – The Bible has given ample warnings, such as: Matthew 3:1-7 (ESV), "In those days John the Baptist came preaching in the wilderness of Judea, Repent, for the kingdom of heaven is at hand...Then Jerusalem and all Judea and all the region about the Jordan were going out to him, and they were baptized by him in the river Jordan, confessing their sins. But when he saw many of the Pharisees and Sadducees coming to his baptism, he said to them, You brood of vipers! Who warned you to flee from the wrath to come?"

Charles Haddon Spurgeon preached a sermon on October 23, 1883 entitled: Flee From The Coming Wrath.

"How do we flee from the coming wrath?

First, we flee from the coming wrath by taking immediate action. You must escape. If you remain where you are now, you will certainly perish. You are in the City of Destruction which is about to be overwhelmed with the fiery flood of the coming wrath. You must be desperate to escape from it before judgment is executed on the place and on everyone who is in it; you must immediately flee from the coming wrath.

Second, Fleeing means, not only immediate action, but swift action. He that flees for his life does not creep and crawl; he runs at his greatest speed, and he wishes that he could ride on the wings of the wind. No pace that he can reach is fast enough for him. Oh, if God the Holy Spirit will make you feel your imminent danger, you will want to fly to Christ with the swiftness of the lightning-flash; you will not be satisfied to linger as you are even for another hour. What if that balcony over there should suddenly collapse on top of you? What if God should give you a fatal stroke while you are still in your sins? What if, in walking home, you should walk into your grave? What if your bed should become your tomb? This may happen to any one of you…so there is no time to linger or delay. Haste is the word for you; God warns you… "Today, if you hear my voice, do not harden your hearts; I tell you, now is the time of My favor, now is the day of salvation" [Hebrews 3:15; 2 Corinthians 6:2].

Third, To flee also means to run directly to your object. A man who flees for his life does not want any indirect, roundabout roads, he takes short cuts, he jumps over hedges and ditches that he may get where he wants to be in the shortest possible time. So going straight to Jesus is the only direction for you. Some people will recommend that you read books, which I am certain you cannot understand, for no living soul can; or perhaps you should meet with persons who want to explain to you some wondrous mystery. Listen to them, if you like, after the great business of

Should Topsy-Turvy Be Cloned?

your salvation is over; but right now you do not have any time for mysteries, you have no time for puzzles, you have no time to be confused and perplexed; the one thing you have to do right now is to run straight to Jesus, straight to Jesus. You are a sinner, and he is the only Savior for sinners; so, trust him, God help you to trust him, and thus to find immediate salvation! You have a severe sin problem, thus you must flee straight to Christ. The plan of salvation is not a thing that is hard to understand. Whoever believes in the Son has eternal life; and they will never be condemned; for they have passed from death to life. There is the gospel in a nutshell; grab hold of it, and live by it. You have no time for anything else, and you have no need of anything else; so flee, flee from the coming wrath.

John the Baptist explained to those Pharisees and Sadducees the way in which they had to flee. He told them, that they must repent. There is no going to heaven by following the road to hell. There is no finding pardon while continuing in sin. Depend upon it, Mr. Drunkard, you will not be forgiven for your drunkenness if you still go on with your drinking. Don't let the man who is immoral imagine that he can go on with his sin and yet be forgiven. Don't let the thief dream that there is any pardon for him unless he quits his evil course, and tries to make restitution as best he can to those he has wronged. There must be repentance.

Second, that repentance must be practical. Note how John put it: Produce fruit in keeping with repentance [Matthew 3:8 - evidences of true repentance is a new life. It is no use feeling sorry for yourself and crying, and praying a prayer of salvation with a lie in your right hand, and then going home to swear and drink, or to avoid Sunday worship, and to live as you like, and all the while still hoping to enter heaven. No, sin and you must part, or else Christ and you can never keep company. Do you remember that message that John Bunyan thought he heard in his head when he was playing sports on Sunday morning. He suddenly stood still with the stick in his hand, for he thought he heard a voice saying to him, "Will you turn away from your sins, and go to heaven, or keep your sins, and go to hell?" That is the alternative which both the law and the gospel put before men and women. "Flee from the coming wrath;" but there is no fleeing from wrath except by repentance of sin, which will be evidenced by the fruits of repentance: a real change of heart and life.

Third, Then John went on to say to the Pharisees and Sadducees that they must give up all the false hopes which they had cherished: "Do not think you can say to yourselves, We have Abraham as our father. Those Pharisees said, in deed, if not in word, It really doesn't matter if we act like hypocrites, for Abraham is our father; and the Sadducees said, in effect, Though we are unbelievers, it is no big thing, for Abraham is our father. No, answered John, you must abandon all such false hopes as that. And if any of you…have said, We will be okay, because we are regular church people, our Mother and Father were good Christian people…your pedigree will avail you nothing unless you personally repent of your sins, and lay hold of Christ as your Savior."

Questions: Are you prepared for That Day? Have you placed your life under the control and authority of Jesus Christ? You would be wise to do it without any further delay.

CONSIDER THESE THINGS WITH ME!

The Pig's Last Oink and Squeal

The Hog has been butchered; the hams have been smoked; the sausage has been ground; the process of making Head Cheese is well underway; and the fat has been rendered - but - the hew and cry is: Bring home more Sausage and Bacon! The demand for more ignores the reality that there is nothing left of the Hog. It might be said that even the hog's squeal went into the Sausage.

The Government's Fiscal Commission held its first meeting and the Daily Caller dated April 28th, 2010 reports: "The pig has died...In such memorable fashion...former Sen. Alan Simpson Tuesday kicked off the U.S. government's effort to keep itself from drowning in debt. Simpson's point was that America is running out of money. Simpson, one of two co-chairs of President Obama's Fiscal Commission, told the 17 other members that during his career in the Senate, his constituents often told him to 'bring home the bacon.' Tuesday's meeting began an attempt – which some think is doomed from the start and others see merely as an exercise to justify higher taxes – to take on America's deficit, debt and runaway entitlement spending. This might be the last best hope to right this listing ship of state of ours, said Simpson, in what was both a warning and a plea. The meeting was full of grave forecasts of disaster if nothing is done to rein in the national debt approaching $13 trillion, deficits that will add to the debt by around $10 trillion over the next decade, and unfunded entitlement spending commitments that Sen. Judd Gregg, New Hampshire Republican, said add up to $66 trillion. The longer we delay, the greater the risk of catastrophic economic consequences, said Robert Reischauer, president of the Urban Institute, who gave testimony and answered questions from the commission....Commission co-chair Erskine Bowles, a former White House chief of staff to President Bill Clinton, said the nation's debt is a cancer ... that is going to destroy our country from within. It's as plain as day - what is really hard is the solution. Rep. Paul Ryan, Wisconsin Republican and ranking member on the House Budget Committee, led the charge to try and focus the commission on cutting spending and not raising taxes. If you look at the math of all of this, spending is the culprit. Mathematically speaking, you literally cannot tax your way out of this problem. Bernanke said that the American people will have to choose among making modifications to entitlement programs such as Medicare and Social Security, restraining federal spending on everything else, accepting higher taxes, or some combination thereof.

The adage cannot be repeated too often: "If your outgo exceeds your income, your upkeep will be your downfall." The Congress of the United States needs to learn some simple definitions and mathematic formulas.

First, define the word Budget. It is: "(a) an estimate of expected income and expense for a given period in the future; (b) a plan of operations based on such an estimate; (c) an itemized allotment of funds for a given period; and (d) the total sum of money set aside or needed for a purpose." This is basic for a family and household and should be for the government.

Secondly, basic mathematics should be utilized. When there was a Gold and Silver Standard in this country, we had a foundation on which the currency and coinage were based. When that was removed as the Standard, then the foundation became the good faith in the American Government (that's when our "word" meant something and wasn't parsed into something vague and meaningless). It was said and meant: Our Word Is Our Bond. Not everyone believes that anymore.

There are Ten Basic Biblical Financial Principles. Some of them are: The first: God is the source of everything. Philippians 4:19 - "My God shall supply all your need according to his riches in glory by Christ Jesus." Proverbs 8:20-21 - "I lead in the way of righteousness…that I may cause those that love me to inherit substance; and I will fill their treasures." "The third is living on a margin. Living on a margin simply means allowing room for things to happen." The fifth: keep out of unnecessary debt. The minute a person goes into debt, he loses a portion of his freedom. As Proverbs 22:7 says, "The rich rules over the poor, and the borrower is servant to the lender." The sixth: learning to be content with what one has. Hebrews 13:5 puts it succinctly: "…be content with such things as ye have: for he hath said, I will never leave you, nor forsake you."

What is it to be Content? Is Contentment occasional or is it continual? How do I or can I know whether or not I have it in my life? Contentment is: peace of mind; mental or emotional satisfaction; mentally or emotionally satisfied with things as they are; assenting to or willing to accept circumstances, a proposed course of action; comfort, happiness.

Several years ago, April 2002, John MacArthur preached a sermon and taught on the subject of Contentment. Among the thoughts are: "Basically if you look at Philippians 4:11, that'll be a good launch point for us. Paul says, "I have learned to be content." I have learned to be content. What a great thing to learn. What a wonderful reality to be content. "Content in whatever circumstances I am." Therefore his contentment was unrelated to those circumstances. At the time that he wrote this he was in the direst of circumstances. He was a prisoner. He was in the worst possible situation.

"…we live in a world that wants to breed discontent. Everything in our society is geared to make you unhappy with your current circumstances: your job, your wardrobe, your car, your house, your wife, place you live, whatever it might be. Everything in the advertising world is designed to breed discontent. To make you unhappy with what you have. Make you miserable with what you have with the current circumstance. And, of course, Satan feeds this because it essentially winds up in the violation and break down of every relationship. And that serves his purpose very well because it's contrary to God's design. So we're living, I think, in a time when we might be able to say that there is a more massive assault on our contentment than in any other time in human history because the sophistication of the attack has never been quite this extreme.

"So I want to talk about this matter of contentment…why Paul was content and how we can be content. But a little bit of background biblically. The psalmist's wrote in Psalm 36:7-8, "How excellent is thy loving kindness, O God, therefore the children of men put their trust under the shadow of thy wings. They shall be abundantly satisfied." There's a synonym for contentment; satisfaction. And the Psalmist said, "That based upon the loving kindness of God, based upon the protection of God we are under the shadow of His wings. He was abundantly satisfied." In Psalm 63:3-5 we read, "Because thy loving kindness is better than life my lips will praise You. Thus will I bless You while I live? I will lift up my hands in Your name. My soul shall be satisfied." Here, again, the psalmist says, "Because of your loving kindness," same thing as we saw in Psalm 36, "because loving kindness means grace, mercy, love, all that's bound up in God's goodness to his own. Because of this," he says, "my soul is satisfied."

"Two psalms later in Psalms 65, the psalmist writes, "We shall be satisfied with the goodness of thy house, O God of our salvation. And then in Psalm 107:9, "He satisfied the longing soul and fills the hungry soul with goodness." And so the Psalmists says that it is part of the longing for the Lord and being under his protection, under his care, under his provision to be satisfied. Contentment is a beautiful word; satisfaction is an equally beautiful word, one that needs emphasis today.

At the very outset of the ministry of Jesus he gave the great Sermon on the Mount. And in that sermon on the mount, Matthew 6:25-35 Jesus said, "For this reason I say to you don't be anxious for your life as to what you shall eat or what you shall drink, nor for your body as to what you shall put on. Is not life more than food and the body than clothing? Look at the birds of the air, they do not sow, neither do they reap nor gather into barns. And, yet, your Heavenly Father feeds them. Are you not worth much more than they? And which of you by being anxious can add a single cubit to his life's span. And why are you anxious about clothing? Observe how the lilies of the field grow. They do not toil nor do they spin. Yet I say to you that even Solomon in all his glory did not clothed himself like one of those. If God so raised the grass of the field, which is alive today and tomorrow is thrown into the furnace, will He not much more do so for you? O men of little faith. Do not be anxious then saying, "What shall we eat or what shall we drink or with what shall we clothe ourselves?" "For all these things the Gentiles eagerly seek for your heavenly Father knows that you have need of all these things. But seek first his Kingdom and His righteousness, and all these things shall be added to you. Therefore, do not be anxious for tomorrow, for tomorrow will take care of itself. Every day has enough trouble of its own."

"Be satisfied today and leave your contentment and your satisfaction for tomorrow to the same God who provides today. This is a righteous kind of contentment."

That's a great and considerable challenge, namely, to begin to implement the Words and Teaching of Jesus Christ making them an integral part of our lives. We err when we think we need more Hog than there is to get. We err when we think someone is denying and depriving us of the last oink and squeal of the butchered hog. Contentment with the Hams and Sausage and Pork Loins, etc. should be evident in us. Much more, this should be evidenced in terms of one's walk and life with the Lord – learning to be content in all situations and every circumstance – because you know God cares for you always. Make contentment your choice!

CONSIDER THESE THINGS WITH ME!

Apple-Carts and Turnovers

In a bygone day in larger cities, there used to be street vendors with push carts where many things were sold. A common item was Fruit and Vegetables. Sometimes, a wheel might come off the cart and it would be upset and the product spilled on the street. A phrase that described such a moment was: "Upsetting The Apple-Cart." The meaning is both simple and obvious, namely, "To cause upset - to create a difficulty." If a wheel came off the cart, or if it was pushed over an unseen hole or obstruction, the cart could turn over. The goods of the merchant, many times fruits and vegetables, would be spilled over the ground and some of them ruined. The origin of the phrase has a political tone to it: This allusory (illusory) phrase is first recorded by Jeremy Belknap in The History of New Hampshire, 1788: "Adams had almost overset the apple-cart by intruding an amendment of his own fabrication on the morning of the day of ratification [of the Constitution]."

When Arizona passed an Immigration Law recently, the reaction was manifold. Not the least of which was: "Mexican President Felipe Calderon has accused Arizona of opening the door to intolerance, hate, discrimination and abuse in law enforcement." That is a fascinating statement, especially in light of Mexican Law and Approach to Immigrants trying to enter Mexico legally or illegally. Michelle Malkin has written (April 2010): How Mexico Treats Illegal Aliens. These regulations and restrictions are imposed on foreigners. Some of the Legal Requirements are: (a) The Mexican government will bar foreigners if they upset "the equilibrium of the national demographics." (b) If outsiders do not enhance the country's "economic or national interests" or are "not found to be physically or mentally healthy," they are not welcome. Neither are those who show "contempt against national sovereignty or security." They must not be economic burdens on society and must have clean criminal histories. Those seeking to obtain Mexican citizenship must show a birth certificate, provide a bank statement proving economic independence, pass an exam and prove they can provide their own healthcare. (c) Illegal entry into the country is equivalent to a felony punishable by two years' imprisonment. Document fraud is subject to fine and imprisonment; so is alien marriage fraud. Evading deportation is a serious crime; illegal re-entry after deportation is punishable by ten years' imprisonment. Foreigners may be kicked out of the country without due process and the endless bites at the litigation apple that illegal aliens are afforded in our country. (d) Law enforcement officials at all levels - by national mandate - must cooperate to enforce immigration laws, including illegal alien arrests and deportations. The Mexican military is also required to assist in immigration enforcement operations. Native-born Mexicans are empowered to make citizens' arrests of illegal aliens and turn them in to authorities. (e) Mexico's National Catalog of Foreigners tracks all outside tourists and foreign nationals. A National Population Registry tracks and verifies the identity of every member of the population, who must carry a citizens' identity card. Visitors who do not possess proper documents and identification are subject to arrest as illegal aliens." She concludes her article with these words: "Mexico is doing the job Arizona is now doing - a job the U.S. government has failed miserably to do: putting its people first. Here's the proper rejoinder to all the hysterical demagogues in Mexico (and their sympathizers here on American soil) now calling for boycotts and invoking Jim Crow laws, apartheid, and the Holocaust because Arizona has taken its sovereignty into its own hands: Hipócritas."

The Bible has several implications and applications regarding aliens. Deuteronomy 24:14-17 gives a basic instruction: "Do not take advantage of a hired man who is poor and needy, whether he is a brother Israelite or an alien living in one of your towns. Pay him his wages each day before sunset...Do not deprive the alien or the fatherless of justice...Remember that you were slaves in Egypt and the Lord your God redeemed you from there…"

Deuteronomy 27 is a listing of "curses" pronounced by The Lord. In verse 19: "Cursed is the man who withholds justice from the alien, the fatherless or the widow. Then all the people shall say, Amen!" The New Testament also makes some "alien and stranger" comment. Hebrews 11:13-15, "All these people…did not receive the things promised…they admitted that they were aliens and strangers on earth." In I Peter 2:11-12, "I urge you, as aliens and strangers in the world, to abstain from sinful desires…Live such good lives among the pagans that…they may see your good deeds and glorify God…"

One of the developing problems in the world is in the area of communication. Language barriers continue to exist. In this multi-lingual world, communication is vital and important. There are far too many languages to learn so translators and linguists are employed in the hope that accurate communication can occur. More than 100 years ago, a means of communication was developed based upon sounds that were transmitted. Most people are knowledgeable in terms of Morse Code. Almost everyone knows that Dot-Dot-Dot, Dash-Dash-Dash, Dot-Dot-Dot stands for SOS (Save Our Ship). Morse Code was originally created for Samuel F. B. Morse's electric telegraph in the early 1840s. Morse code was also extensively used for early radio communication beginning in the 1890s. In the early part of the twentieth century, the majority of high-speed international communication was conducted in Morse code, using telegraph lines, undersea cables, and radio circuits. Morse code is a type of character encoding that transmits telegraphic information using rhythm. Morse code uses a standardized sequence of short and long elements to represent the letters, numerals, punctuation and special characters of a given message. The short and long elements can be formed by sounds, marks, or pulses, in on off keying and are commonly known as "dots" and "dashes" or "dits" and "dahs". The speed of

Morse code is measured in words per minute (WPM) or characters per minute.

It's fascinating to read a recently published article: "People All Across The World Are Discovering Numerous Ways To Communicate" By Jeff Winkler in The Daily Caller on 04/29/10. He writes: "In London, a translation firm has posted an ad on Craigslist seeking freelance translators. They're not interested in Chinese, Italian or even Swahili speakers. They need people who speak Brooklynese. According to the New York Daily News: The freelance gig pays up to $210 a day. It's open to anyone who can decipher such Brooklynisms as "not for nothin,'" "cawfee" and "whatayagonna do? We're looking for someone who loves the dialect and is able to understand someone who has the heaviest Brooklyn accent, said Mick Thorburn, spokesman for Today Translations…The most amazing story of the day comes from The Daily Mail, which is reporting that a blind boy has acquired his sight by learning a different language. To be clear, the language is dolphin…Young Jamie Aspland utters tiny high-pitch clicks to rebound the sound off surfaces and guide him round obstacles. The four-year-old who was born without his sight was taught the echo location technique as part of an exciting technique pioneered in the U.S to help the blind. He copied the technique dolphins used to navigate their way through the murky depths – using high pitch clicks to penetrate objects and reflect off their internal structure. Jamie is able to mirror that behavior, which complements his use of a cane, by flicking his tongue against the roof of his mouth to mimic the porpoise's underwater tones. Little Jamie still hasn't decided what he wants to be when he grows up. He's narrowed it down to Dr. Doolittle or The Daredevil."

There was a time when there was just one language in the world. Genesis 11:1-9 gives the account of when and why multiple languages came into being. The text states: "The whole world had one language and a common speech. As men moved eastward, they found a plain in Shinar and settled there. They said to each other, Come, let's make bricks and bake them thoroughly. They used brick instead of stone, and tar for mortar. Then they said, let us build ourselves a city, with a tower that reaches to the heavens, so that we may make a name for ourselves and not be scattered over the face of the whole earth. But the Lord came down to see the city and the tower that the men were building. The Lord said, If as one people speaking the same language they have begun to do this, then nothing they plan to do will be impossible for them...let us go down and confuse their language so they will not understand each other. So the Lord scattered them from there over all the earth, and they stopped building the city. That is why it was called Babel - because there the Lord confused the language of the whole world..." One of the instigators of this plan was Nimrod (his name means: "Let Us Revolt"). Today, finding ways and means to communicate clearly and accurately is a challenge and need. And yet, The Bible reminds us that "Actions Speak Louder Than Words." In I John 3:18, "...let us not love with words or tongue but with actions and in truth."

Don't let anyone or anything Upset Your Apple-Cart or cause it to Turnover. Don't let anyone or anything deter you from being a viable communication link to others in our world. The Alien and stranger – could it be that The Lord is bringing a Mission Field to your doorstep? Up to this point, have you missed or misunderstood what God is doing and what He wants you to do? If we implement - "...let us not love with words or tongue but with actions and in truth." we can easily get beyond merely Click-Click Communication and other barriers. At the very least, let's try!

CONSIDER THESE THINGS WITH ME!

Expectations Versus Abilities

As events unfold in ones life, sooner or later reference will be made to "The Peter Principle"! The general interpretation is that a person has a level of ability/competency and to go beyond that level invokes The Peter Principle. What is The Peter Principle? The Peter Principle states that in a hierarchy every employee tends to rise to his/her level of incompetence. It was formulated by Dr. Laurence J. Peter and Raymond Hull in their 1968 book The Peter Principle, a humorous treatise which also introduced the salutary science of Hierarchiology, inadvertently founded by Peter, the principle has real validity. It holds that in a hierarchy, members are promoted so long as they work competently. Sooner or later they are promoted to a position at which they are no longer competent (their level of incompetence), and there they remain. Peter's corollary states that in time, every post tends to be occupied by an employee who is incompetent to carry out his duties and adds that work is accomplished by those employees who have not yet reached their level of incompetence.

The Author, Gary North, in his Thesis: "Computers Versus The Peter Principle" writes: "The Peter Principle vies with Parkinson's Law as one of the two most fundamental laws of bureaucracy. Parkinson's Law was first articulated in public in 1955: Work expands so as to fill the time available for its completion. C. Northcote Parkinson was a professional historian with the famous dry wit that was once common to the British upper class. He turned an article in The Economist into a book, Parkinson's Law, in 1957. He later offered a corollary: "Expenditure rises to meet income. The Peter Principle was first made public in Jan. 1967, in an article in Esquire. This principle announces: In a hierarchy, every employee tends to rise to his level of incompetence. Professor Peter was a specialist in the area of hierarchical incompetence. He was a professor of education. Here is his thesis. People get promoted in a hierarchy for as long as they display competence on the job. At some point, however, everyone hits his ceiling of competence. But neither he nor his employer recognizes that this is his top. So, he is given one additional promotion. At that point, he has risen to his level of incompetence. He will cease receiving any further promotions."

While there are many applications that can be made in this regard, rather than drift toward denigrating any group, the point of focus is on motivation, skills development, ability that matches expectation, and maximized performance. A reason why Seminars and In-Service Training has been developed is to hone the skills of an individual so there can be increased motivation, skill development, productivity and realization of fulfillment in ones task. Regardless of ones experience and task involvement, there is considerable development in all skill areas. It would be shortsighted and unwise to ignore or be detached from the opportunities to increase knowledge and to learn better ways to accomplish a task. It is possible to invent a better mouse trap, or a better broom, etc. The learning curve is always a continuum and maximum potential is always the pursuit. None of this can occur through osmosis! It requires discipline and study and effort.

The Peter Principle is shattered when the Spiritual Dynamic enters. God, The Creator, spoke – "Let Us Make" – and the Universe and Man came into being. Two thoughts: In Matthew 4:18, as Jesus began to summon men/disciples, He said: "Come, follow me…and I will make you…" It would be instilling extraordinary skills and abilities into ordinary men. In like manner, in II Corinthians 5:17, we read: "…if anyone is in Christ, he/she is a new creation; the old has gone, the new has come!" The operative phrase is "new creation"! The overall point is that God has always been The Creator and His Work is now particularized in terms of the one who is In Christ. There is a new horizon, a new hope, a new potential, a new "You" as this new creation takes place, and the words of Jesus echo to you – "I Will Make You…" into what I want you to be. The only way this proposition can be proven and tested is for one to be In Christ where this new creation process will take place. To read about this "new creation" possibility further, one can consult Psalm 1; Ephesians 2 and 4; II Corinthians 5; etc. The difference between The Peter Principle and The Jesus Principle is that Jesus guarantees the new creation result in and for you!

However, in the government of and by men, polarization is a reality and conflict resolution is difficult to achieve. For instance, it's obvious that polarization (a sharp division, as of a population or group, into opposing factions) is a reality within our nation. In an effort to address conflict on a secular level, someone has developed a list of 8 Possibilities For Conflict Resolution as a starting point:

1. Know Yourself and Your Vulnerabilities – Take Care of Yourself So You Don't Capitulate Inappropriately Just To Achieve Resolve At Any Cost;
2. Clarify Personal Needs Threatened By Dispute or Misunderstanding;
3. Identify A Safe and Neutral Place for Discussion or Negotiation;
4. Be Ready To Listen As Well As To Interact;
5. Assert Your Needs Calmly, Clearly and Specifically;
6. Approach Problem-Solving and Conflict Resolution with Flexibility;
7. Manage Impasse with Gentleness, Patience, and Respect;
8. Develop A Realistic Agreement that Can Result In Mutual Resolve.

These steps should be able to begin a conversation and dialogue between individuals and/or groups. There are some "impasse" circumstances (a position or situation from which there is no escape; resolute deadlock) that make any effort challenging and difficult. Many Divorce Circumstances have reached the "Impasse" level before counsel is sought or desired. The ongoing conflict between Israel and Hamas (Gaza) represents a situation of great concern but one that is not ripe for resolution at this moment. One has to search to find those moments of national unity within our own nation – such moments, like September 11, 2001, evaporate all too quickly and the nation reverts back to its polarizing body politic. One wonders - ponders: Can Peace – Will Peace ever be a national reality again?

In a NEWSMAX Article (December 23rd, 2008), Jim Walters reported: U.S. Military Preparing For Domestic Disturbances. The report contains the following: "A new report from the U.S. Army War College discusses the use of American troops to quell civil unrest brought about by a worsening economic crisis. The report from the War College's Strategic Studies Institute warns that the U.S. military must prepare for a violent, strategic dislocation inside the United States that could be provoked by unforeseen economic collapse or loss of functioning political and legal order...Widespread civil violence inside the United States would force the defense establishment to reorient priorities in extremis to defend basic domestic order...An American government and defense establishment lulled into complacency by a long-secure domestic order would be forced to rapidly divest some or most external security commitments in order to address rapidly expanding human insecurity at home. International Monetary Fund Managing Director...warned...of riots and unrest in global markets if the ongoing financial crisis is not addressed and lower-income households are beset with credit constraints and rising unemployment, the Phoenix Business Journal reported. Sen. James Inhofe of Oklahoma and Rep. Brad Sherman of California disclosed that then Treasury Secretary Henry Paulson discussed a worst-case scenario as he pushed the Wall Street bailout in September 2008, and said that scenario might even require a declaration of martial law. The Army College report states: DOD might be forced by circumstances to put its broad resources at the disposal of civil authorities to contain and reverse violent threats to domestic tranquility. Under the most extreme circumstances, this might include use of military force against hostile groups inside the United States..." It's frightening to contemplate how the government is thinking in it's secret enclaves and behind closed doors. The worst-case scenarios and possible chaos are disturbing.

A Functional Axiom for life and governing is: "It's never right to do wrong so that right can occur." The Biblical Approach is simply (Psalm 122:6-9): "Pray for the peace of Jerusalem (or Washington, DC, etc.): May those who love you be secure. May there be peace within your walls and security within your citadels. For the sake of my brothers and friends, I will say, Peace be within you. For the sake of the house of the Lord our God, I will seek your prosperity." It is a focus away from self-serving interests and wants to a collective consideration – what is best overall and will serve the best interests of the greater number. Additionally (Psalm 34:11-14), "Come, my children, listen to me; I will teach you the fear of the Lord. Whoever of you loves life and desires to see many good days, keep your tongue from evil and your lips from speaking lies. Turn from evil and do good; seek peace and pursue it." These are first-steps on the path and road to Conflict Resolution and the lessening of Polarization. Try It! You Might Like It!

CONSIDER THESE THINGS WITH ME!

Dispossessing God

All too soon (in the year 2026), the United States of America will mark the 250th year of existence as a free and independent nation. This nation has been preserved through good times and bad times. We have endured several wars, including two World Wars. We were victimized by two surprise attacks – Pearl Harbor on December 7, 1941 and sixty (60) years later on September 11, 2001. We have passed through recessions and depressions and recovered very well. As a nation, we should remember, learn, and be encouraged by our history and our resilience. In like manner, we should be warned by complacency and compromises that have contributed to our cultural demise and ongoing struggle.

Who would have thought that the efforts of one determined woman in June of 1963 would cause the Supreme Court of the United States to alter the cultural and religious heritage of this nation? On that date, the United States Supreme Court upheld the argument of the atheist Madelyn Murray O'Hare and promulgated an edict with ramifications so widespread it insured that God would be evicted from public society across the entire spectrum of the American governmental system. From that day to this, not only has prayer been outlawed, God's very name has been declared anathema to the United States Constitution, and forbidden to be mentioned in any federal, state, county, city or municipal context. Further decrees have revealed the depths of the Dispossessing of God that initial edict fostered. Not just Bible Reading, but prayer, the display of the cross, the Ten Commandments, Nativity Scenes/Presentations are disallowed, etc.

On the Eve of the Inauguration of the 44th President of the United States, this same controversy is brought to bear and formal court appeals are being made by Atheists in our nation. Prayer is alright only if one does not use the name of God and In Jesus' Name. The Oath of Office can say whatever, just so long as it does not conclude with four words, namely, "so help me God." One Pundit on a Sunday News Program allowed that the Ceremonial use of God has become so diminished that it is merely a term without significance.

If that is true, and it certainly appears that it is, we have come too far as a nation and may not have much further to go. A nation that Dispossesses God is a nation charting a course toward difficulty, judgment and obliteration.

It's no wonder the effort has been made to remove the Bible from the public arena. There are some Warning Signs regarding the nation that is indifferent and/or ignores God. Note the following Scriptural teaching:

II Thessalonians 2:3-4[NLT], "Don't be fooled…that day will not come until there is a great rebellion against God and the man of lawlessness is revealed – the one who brings destruction. He will exalt himself and defy every god there is and tear down every object of adoration and worship. He will position himself in the temple of God, claiming that he himself is God."

There are always Signs and Warnings along life's road if only they are read and heeded. Think back to the 1963 Supreme Court Decision and link that banning of God to some events warned about in Scripture…

Jeremiah 44:28-30 states: "…Then all those who came to Egypt will find out whose words are true, mine or theirs! And this is the proof I give you, says the LORD, that all I have threatened will happen to you and that I will punish you here: I will turn Pharaoh…king of Egypt, over to his enemies who want to kill him…" Following the 1963 Court Ruling, there were three Assassinations in our nation! Coincidence? Or, a Warning Sign!

Matthew 24:6-9, Jesus stated: "…wars will break out near and far, but don't panic. Yes, these things must come, but the end won't follow immediately. The nations and kingdoms will proclaim war against each other, and there will be famines and earthquakes in many parts of the world. But all this will be only the beginning of the horrors to come. Earthquakes and Tidal Waves and Wars - Coincidence? Or, A Warning Sign!

Jeremiah 51:41-43, "...How Babylon is fallen – great Babylon, praised throughout the earth! The world can scarcely believe its eyes at her fall! The sea has risen over Babylon; she is covered by its waves. Her cities now lie in ruins; she is a dry wilderness where no one lives or even passes by." Tsunami – Coincidence? Or, A Warning Sign!

There are very practical warning signs that seem to gain the attention of people. It makes one wonder whether or not people are listening and observing. Are they concerned? Do they care? Is indifference the attitude of our times? Have we chosen to be duped rather than being alert to the times in which we live?

The US Senate is beginning to look like a Mental Institution that has been taken over by the patients – there is so little order, decorum or common sense on display there currently. An example is a Newsday Article (January 8th,, 2009) regarding: "Senate Democratic leaders yesterday laid out a path for former Illinois Attorney General Roland Burris to replace President-elect Barack Obama in the Senate, softening their initial ardent opposition to Burris' appointment last week. After an hour-long meeting with Burris on Capitol Hill, Sen. Majority Leader Harry Reid of Nevada and Majority Whip Richard Durbin of Illinois told reporters that they would consider Burris' appointment if it is certified by the Illinois secretary of state and if Burris testifies successfully before legislators in Illinois who are considering the impeachment of Democratic Gov. Rod Blagojevich, who is accused of corruption charges, including looking to sell Obama's Senate seat. Once that's done, we'll be in a position to see what we're going to do, said Reid, who last week had declared any appointment that Blagojevich made would be tainted. In a news conference yesterday morning, Obama said he would accept Burris as his replacement in the Senate." The List of things for Mr. Burris "to do" if he is to be considered is bogus and a face-saving procedure to cover-over the foolishness of the Senate Majority Leader. It is part of the game people often play in Washington, DC.

This reminded me of a "to do List" suggested by Max Lucado in his book, In The Eye Of The Storm. He speaks of various "lists" that people could and should consider for their lives. Among his suggestions are: "The Bible certainly has its share of lists. Moses brought one down from the mountain. There are lists of the gifts of the Spirit. Lists of good fruit and bad. Lists of salutations and greetings…." Then he shares a long list of "to do" things.

- Love God more than you fear hell.
- Once a week, let a child take you on a walk.
- Make major decisions in a cemetery.
- When no one is watching, live as if someone is.
- Succeed at home first.
- Don't spend tomorrow's money today.
- Pray twice as much as you fret.
- Listen twice as much as you speak.
- Only harbor a grudge when God does.
- Never outgrow your love of sunsets.
- Treat people like angels; you will meet some and help make some.
- It's wiser to err on the side of generosity than on the side of scrutiny.
- God has forgiven you; you'd be wise to do the same.
- When you can't trace God's hand, trust his heart.
- Toot your own horn and the notes will be flat.
- Don't feel guilty for God's goodness.

- The book of life is lived in chapters, so know your page number.
- Never let the important be the victim of the trivial.
- Live your liturgy.
- Approach life like a voyage on a schooner. Enjoy the view. Explore the vessel. Make friends with the Captain.

Guidelines and suggestions are only valid if they are implemented. A pithy statement from the past states: "God has given you two ears and one mouth – he expects you to do twice as much listening as you do talking." That's the idea shared in James 1:19 (NLT): "My dear brothers and sisters, be quick to listen, slow to speak, and slow to get angry." Elected officials surely need to put those words into practice – but then – so do you and I.

Have you…we…I been diligent in trying it? I didn't think so! One would do well to think about these things and to give heed to them!

CONSIDER THESE THINGS WITH ME!

Unimaginable and Unprecedented

Generalization is a tool in expression that allows one to either overstate or underestimate what is or is not factual. Every year, a week will be observed as National Right To Life Week. An example is this statement appearing on www.OneNewsNow.com - "Less than 10% believe abortion should be legal, unfettered...A nationwide survey commissioned by the U.S. Conference of Catholic Bishops underscores the public view of abortion. The poll involved a cross-section of Americans - not just Catholics - and assistant director for policy and communications at the U.S. Conference of Catholic Bishops, Deirdre McQuade, has part of the results. "Four out of five American adults - 82 percent - think abortion should be either illegal under all circumstances or with limited legality, and only nine percent said that abortion should be legal for any reason at any time during pregnancy, she explains." The report also includes: "Three-fourths favor parents having a role in a minor's attempt to obtain an abortion, and nearly two-thirds support laws against partial-birth abortion."

Chuck Colson shared some of his thoughts on the Right To Life Issue and commented in a recent Breakpoint editorial: "In the painting The Slaughter of the Innocents, baroque artist Peter Paul Rubens depicted the horror: a soldier dashing a child against a Roman column, another lancing a mother who tries to hide her babe. The painting also shows a woman weeping over the body of her dead infant. It's a scene from the Bible none of us likes imagining. Matthew quoted Jeremiah to describe the atrocity: A voice is heard in Ramah... Rachel weeping for her children and refusing to be comforted... Those who heard Matthew's gospel...would have associated Ramah with the deportation of the Jews during the exile. In that vicinity, the Babylonians tore Israel's children away from their mother's arms and carried them off as slaves." As barbaric as this sounds, much of what passes as a safe and sound medical procedure when Abortion is done in this nation, is similarly barbaric. Colson's additional thoughts are: "And where did Evil strike? It attacked life in its most vulnerable form. The very first assault of Satan after the birth of Christ is against society's weakest members - infants. He attacked the least of these.

Even today, the Enemy's mode of attack hasn't changed much. We're painfully aware of the slaughter of the unborn, and the devaluation of the elderly, the poor, the disabled, and the prisoner...we mustn't be deceived. There is a real battle with real casualties. We remember that we wage war not against flesh and blood, but against the rulers, against the authorities, against the powers of this dark world and against the spiritual forces of evil in the heavenly realms. We shouldn't be surprised at setbacks and assaults upon us. Of course the Enemy won't go down without a fight. But remember, the Kingdom of Heaven has been forcefully advancing, and forceful men lay hold of it. So lay hold of it, and don't let go.

The secular press will brush aside such statements as being either biased or uninformed. That is part of the tension/dynamic of a juggernaut approach on the one hand (a massive inexorable force that seems to crush everything in its way) versus those who embrace a view and/or position that becomes nothing more than a foible: (a minor weakness or failing of character.)"...What should matter most to us is a Biblical imperative to be involved in the Cultural War that engages us as followers of Jesus Christ. Remember Proverbs 24:10-12, " If you falter in times of trouble, how small is your strength! Rescue those being led away to death; hold back those staggering toward slaughter. If you say, But we knew nothing about this, does not He Who weighs the heart perceive it? Does not He Who guards your life know it? Will he not repay each person according to what he has done?" And, Psalm 139:7-16, "... For You created my inmost being; You knit me together in my mother's womb. I praise You because I am fearfully and wonderfully made; Your works are wonderful, I know that full well. My frame was not hidden from You when I was made in the secret place. When I was woven together in the depths of the earth, Your eyes saw my unformed body. All the days ordained for me were written in Your book before one of them came to be. How precious to me are Your thoughts, O God! How vast is the sum of them!" The bottom line for us is – and always will be – God's Way or man's way. These positions are an eternity apart!

Can anything be done that will impact the views in this nation regarding abortion? Is it a hopeless mission and challenge? Should we just accept things as they are and no longer be engaged in the right to life of these unborn infants? Do we deem this to be too steep of a hill to climb and that it will only lead to frustration and conflict? Is it to be relegated to that which though to be impossible?

Years ago, based on the words of Matthew 19:26 - "Jesus looked at them and said, With man this is impossible, but with God all things are possible." - Eugene L. Clark penned the words to a meaningful Inspirational Chorus. The words are:

> Nothing is impossible when you put your trust in God;
> Nothing is impossible when you're trusting in His Word.
> Hearken to the voice of God to thee;
> Is there anything too hard for Me?
> Then put your trust in God alone and rest upon His Word;
> For everything, O, everything,
> yes everything is possible with God.

Amid all the Pomp and Circumstance that surrounds the Inauguration of a President of the United States, there continues to be the relentless hew and cry of all types of people expressing opposition to praying "in Jesus' name…"; or in the Oath of Office to state the words – "so help me God…"etc. If there's anything that illustrates how the United States has drifted into a post-Christian era, this concerted effort by the Atheists and

Humanists and Gay Activists speak volumes. Is it possible that we are approaching, or are at, the day Jesus warned about in Matthew 24:9-12, "You will be hated by all nations because of Me. At that time many will turn away from the faith and will betray and hate each other, and many false prophets will appear and deceive many people. Because of the increase of wickedness, the love of most will grow cold, but he who stands firm to the end will be saved..."

Despite where we may find ourselves in the geo-political turmoil and economic crises of such great magnitude, we continue to have a God-given responsibility to activate I Timothy 2:1-4, "I urge, then, first of all, that requests, prayers, intercession and thanksgiving be made for everyone--for kings and all those in authority, that we may live peaceful and quiet lives in all godliness and holiness. This is good, and pleases God our Savior, who wants all men to be saved and to come to knowledge of the truth."

And even in the most difficult circumstances, I Peter 2:13-17 instructs and urges that we – "Submit yourselves for the Lord's sake to every authority instituted among men: whether to the king, as the supreme authority, or to governors, who are sent by him to punish those who do wrong and to commend those who do right. For it is God's will that by doing good you should silence the ignorant talk of foolish men. Live as free men, but do not use your freedom as a cover-up for evil; live as servants of God. Show proper respect to everyone: Love the brotherhood of believers, fear God, honor the king."

It may involve and entail assuming the role of Moses, Elijah, Daniel and his Friends, or John the Baptist as one takes a stand for righteousness. We must guard against being trapped in the whirlpool of indifference or the malaise of matter-of-factness. As you live in an unfocused world, you must maintain the true focus as you walk and live and sing throughout your life.

> Then put your trust in God alone
> and rest upon His Word;

For everything, O, everything,
yes everything is possible with God.

Do we really believe the premise that Nothing Is Impossible with God?

There have been several people in history who have made an effort to do what no one else had done before. One such feat was for someone to walk across Niagara Falls on a Tightrope. Niagara Falls lying on the border of Ontario, Canada, and New York State is a spectacular scene and is a formidable challenge for any man. Can the Falls be safely crossed by a man? Is it possible?

The first of many tightrope walkers to cross the Falls was Jean Francois Gravelot, a French aerialist, who called himself The Great Blondin, because of his fair hair. He was born February 28, 1824 in St. Omer, Pas de Calais in Northern France. Blondin had been walking the tightrope since the age of five. He was orphaned at age nine. He became a famous tightrope performer and practiced each new feat until he could perform it with his eyes closed. In 1851, at the age of twenty-seven, he joined the Ravel troupe of French equestrian and acrobatic performers on their tour of North American. By this time there were no acrobatic performances at which he did not excel. About Niagara Falls, Blondin, said, "To cross the roaring waters became the ambition of my life."

On June 30, 1859, Blondin made his first journey across the Falls. For this crossing, Blondin utilized a 1,300 foot long , 3 inch diameter manila rope stretched from what is now Prospect Park in Niagara Falls, New York to what is now Oakes Garden in Niagara Falls, Ontario. He began his first walk from the American side and completed his crossing in 20 minutes. Blondin used a thirty-foot long balancing pole that weighed 40 pounds. He stepped onto the tightrope and started his long descent down the cable, which, at midpoint, was fifty feet lower over the gorge. There he stopped, dropped a bottle tied a piece of twine into the

Maid of the Mist tourist boat below, hauled up some Niagara River water, drank it, and resumed his journey, uphill this time. He arrived on the far bank triumphant, though bathed in sweat. He rested briefly and then walked back across in just eight minutes.

That which was thought to be impossible was demonstrated to be possible. It required that a man would be willing to risk everything to accomplish what no one had been able to do before – he was the first.

In life's experiences, there are moments and situations that one can easily be placed into the category of the impossible. In matters of faith and practice, there are situations and moments that are thought to be impossible. However, are they? Are you one who is willing to risk everything to try to do what everyone else may be saying is foolish or impossible?

What will it take to begin the adventure of accomplishing the impossible in Jesus Name? How can the unimaginable and the unprecedented become a reality?

Matthew 17:20, Jesus replied - "Because you have so little faith. I tell you the truth, if you have faith as small as a mustard seed, you can say to this mountain, Move from here to there and it will move. Nothing will be impossible for you."

Do you believe the words of Jesus? Will you take the first step on the tightrope of faith?

CONSIDER THESE THINGS WITH ME!

Tulipomania and Hoopla

Tulipomania = "A violent passion for the acquisition or cultivation of tulips" -- In Holland, in the first half of the 17th century, the cultivation of tulips became a mania. It began about the year 1634, and, like a violent epidemic, seized upon all classes of the community, leading to disasters and misery such as the records of commerce or of bankruptcies can scarcely parallel. In 1636, tulip marts had been established in Amsterdam, Rotterdam, Haarlem, Leyden, and various other towns, where tulip bulbs were sold and resold in the same manner as stocks are on the Stock Exchange of London.

Hoopla = "Boisterous, jovial commotion or excitement; Extravagant publicity; Talk intended to mislead or confuse…" A play by Shakespeare entitled: "MUCH ADO ABOUT NOTHING" - The main plot in Much Ado About Nothing is the same as the story of Ariodante and Ginevra in Ariosto; but the secondary circumstances and development are very different. The mode in which the innocent Hero before the altar at the moment of the wedding, and in the presence of her family and many witnesses, is put to shame by the most degrading charge, false indeed, yet clothed with every appearance of truth, is a grand piece of theatrical effect in the true and justifiable sense…" This Title – Much Ado About Nothing - has been varied along the way until it recently was used in reference to the final episode of The Jerry Seinfeld Show when it became Much Adieu About Nothing. Observers noted: "How important is the last episode to American televiewers? A 30-second commercial spot costs $1,500,000. A 35-foot-high screen was erected in Times-Square to carry the event, while negotiations were taking place to televise the show on a giant screen to 500,000 viewers in Central Park. The Smithsonian Institute in Washington made inquiries about obtaining the entire set of Seinfeld. It was the climax of a show which people said defines our generation, and is the quintessential identification of the '90s. It was a final judgment built on nine years of hype (hope's replacement in a world of synthetic images). It was, as some said, a national holiday."

Misplaced Values and Cultural Saturation with Minutia bring one to the threshold of "hype" versus bona fide "hope"! In other words, we have delved into Fiction and Fantasy to such a degree that we are unable to find authenticity. It brings nations to a place where it allows lofty rhetoric to super-impose itself where bottom-line factualness has become a void. This occurs across all strata of culture and life until we reach the point of "hype" replacing (or becoming) "hope" – and – authenticity is deliberately blurred to smooth the way for adoption of a new agenda. As a result "right to an abortion" becomes "pro-Choice"; "redistribution of wealth" (welfare) becomes "reinvestment"; etc.

During the earth-ministry of the Lord Jesus Christ, many times he would employ a word or phrase – "Verily, Verily, I say unto you…" VERILY means: In truth; in fact; With confidence; assuredly…" Some examples are: John 5:24 Verily, verily, I say unto you, He that hears my word, and believeth on him that sent me, hath everlasting life, and shall not come into condemnation; but is passed from death unto life. Matthew 5:18 For verily I say unto you, Till heaven and earth pass, one jot or one tittle shall in no wise pass from the law, till all be fulfilled. Matthew 18:3 And said, Verily I say unto you, Except ye be converted, and become as little children, ye shall not enter into the kingdom of heaven. John 6:47 Verily, verily, I say unto you, He that believeth on me hath everlasting life. Matthew 26:21 And as they did eat, he said, Verily I say unto you, that one of you shall betray me. Attention and commitment should be placed in what is factual – the Verily – words of The One Who stated: "I am the way; the truth; and the life! No one comes to the Father except by Me!" Tulipomania can bring about a "herd instinct" where people will be caught up by the rhetoric and miss the authentic. Hoopla is what it suggests – much activity and lofty platitudes – but – very little result and great disappointment regarding what one "hoped" would be when the "hype" was innocently embraced.

The misplaced hope reminds one of a bygone as a child growing up in New York City. Amidst all of the rush from place to place there were places where one could pause for refreshment or a fast meal. There were several places such as Nedick's where one could buy Orange Juice, Coffee, a Donut or a Hot Dog with Mustard. The cost was minimal and the refreshment was usually tasty. For a little bit more of a luxury, there was Horn and Hardart Automat. These cafeterias featured prepared foods behind small glass windows and coin-operated slots, beginning with buns, beans, fish cakes and coffee. Eventually, they served lunch and dinner entrees, such as beef stew and Salisbury steak with mashed potatoes. The self-service restaurants operated in the city for nearly a century. They would also offer sandwiches and different desserts. One would deposit a specified number of nickels into a slot and a window would be released to allow one to slide out the food preference. It was a fast-food place with minimum bedlam. It wasn't long before Push Carts were on street corners selling Hot Dogs with ample Sauer Kraut and Mustard.

Somewhere in the 1950's, Baskin-Robbins started Ice Cream Franchises that featured 31 different flavors. Even though the Chain is somewhat diminished from its peak popularity, where it continues to be operational, they advertise and boast of now having more than 1,000 flavors. Some of us grew up being very content with Vanilla, Chocolate or Strawberry – but – that was then and this is now. Carvel Frozen Custard was a similar chain offering a different kind of frozen dessert. There were also the Good Humor Trucks who sold Ice Cream Bars for 10 cents, whereas a competitor name Bungalow Bar sold their Ice Cream Bars for 5 cents.

It seems as though the Baskin-Robbins Concept has become engaged in other parts of our experience ranging from the food choices available, to the religious variants, and the changing political climes. During the Inaugural Prayer Service for President Obama, when a Unity Prayer was being offered, it seemed as though it was a type of Religious Cross-Cultural Seminar. There was a range of prayers from an Orthodox Jewish Rabbi to a Hamas sympathizer to a TV Preacher (T.D. Jakes) attempting to quote from Star Wars and calling it Star Trek, when he said: "I say to you as my son who is here today, my 14-year-old son - he probably would not quote scripture. He probably would use Star Trek instead, and so I say, 'May the force be with you." In the name of being contemporary and relevant, the misquote also represents a missed opportunity to stand tall and represent clearly that all-power belongs to the Eternal God and He allows one to temporarily have a portion of power to work in the affairs of State and to lead in a righteous way.

Where was the prayer suggesting the words of Proverbs 14:34, "Righteousness exalts a nation, but sin is a disgrace/reproach to any people…" – to offset the Inaugural Benediction of a weary and hackneyed civil rights proponent (Joseph Lowery) who prayed: "Lord, in the memory of all the saints who from their labors rest, and in the joy of a new beginning, we ask you to help us work for that day when black will not be asked to get in back, when brown can stick around… when the red man can get ahead, man; and when white will embrace what is right. That all those who do justice and love mercy say Amen. Say Amen!" Only in America can one view a Political and Historic event – The Inauguration of A President – while at the same time being exposed to an ecumenical hodge-podge of religious hoopla and talking (prayer?) points?! Where was any appeal to walk humbly with God and for righteousness that would exalt the nation?

As clergy were caught up in the euphoria of the moment, there were missed opportunities to represent The Almighty God and Truth. Where was the alternative word regarding the movement toward a Tax Rebate for all Americans – even the more than 40% who pay no taxes at all – with the word from God, "If a man doesn't work – neither should he eat." (This does not suggest or imply that people groups should starve to death! What it is

Tulipomania and Hoopla

suggesting is that people need to be motivated to be diligent and productive – becoming a people who can arrive at a point where they can share with others rather than conniving to receive from "the system"!) It's an idea the Apostle Paul shared in II Corinthians 9:10-12, "Now he who supplies seed to the sower and bread for food will also supply and increase your store of seed and will enlarge the harvest of your righteousness. You will be made rich in every way so that you can be generous on every occasion, and through us your generosity will result in thanksgiving to God. This service that you perform is not only supplying the needs of God's people but is also overflowing in many expressions of thanks to God."

It is one thing to embrace I Corinthians 9:22-23, "I have become all things to all men so that by all possible means I might save some. I do all this for the sake of the gospel..." as a purpose for one's life mission. It is entirely another matter when one promises that the government will provide for everything a person or family needs to survive and progress in this nation and world. The Baskin-Robbins approach is incapable of providing enough flavor selection to please and satisfy every appetite. The short-sightedness is the idea that Government will do what only the Grace of Almighty God can accomplish, namely, II Corinthians 9:6-8, "Remember this: Whoever sows sparingly will also reap sparingly, and whoever sows generously will also reap generously. Each man should give what he has decided in his heart to give, not reluctantly or under compulsion, for God loves a cheerful giver. And God is able to make all grace abound to you, so that in all things at all times, having all that you need, you will abound in every good work." Quite a difference – but then – quite an Excellent God Who will do it!

It's obvious we have lost our way as a nation. We seem to have become indifferent to the things of God. We can go through religious motions without having any clear focus or a matching faith with expectation that there is a God Who is hearing, as well as One Who is observing all our deeds and all our actions. We have distanced and desensitized ourselves from The God Who cares deeply and greatly about being demeaned and ignored.

The potpourri of Inaugural Prayers and the chosen lifestyles of our fellow-citizens reminds one of the words in Isaiah 1:15-20 – "When you spread out your hands, I will hide my eyes from you; even though you make many prayers, I will not listen; your hands are full of blood. Wash yourselves; make yourselves clean; remove the evil of your deeds from before my eyes; cease to do evil, learn to do good; seek justice, correct oppression; bring justice to the fatherless, plead the widow's cause. Come now, let us reason together, says the Lord: though your sins are like scarlet, they shall be as white as snow; though they are red like crimson, they shall become like wool. If you are willing and obedient, you shall eat the good of the land; but if you refuse and rebel, you shall be eaten by the sword; for the mouth of the Lord has spoken." God means what he has issued in His Word. Are you ready to acknowledge and honor Him?

CONSIDER THESE THINGS WITH ME!

Matters of the Heart

A Sunday School Teacher impressed upon us the need to keep before us Proverbs 4:23 – 27, "Keep your heart with all vigilance, for from it flow the springs of life. Put away from you crooked speech and put devious talk far from you. Let your eyes look directly forward, and your gaze be straight before you. Ponder the path of your feet; then all your ways will be sure. Do not swerve to the right or to the left; turn your foot away from evil." The paraphrase in The Message translation is very succinct – "Keep vigilant watch over your heart; that's where life starts. Don't talk out of both sides of your mouth; avoid careless banter, white lies, and gossip. Keep your eyes straight ahead; ignore all sideshow distractions. Watch your step, and the road will stretch out smooth before you. Look neither right nor left; leave evil in the dust." The New Living Translation is also very clear and plain – "Above all else, guard your heart, for it affects everything you do. Avoid all perverse talk; stay far from corrupt speech. Look straight ahead, and fix your eyes on what lies before you. Mark out a straight path for your feet; then stick to the path and stay safe. Don't get sidetracked; keep your feet from following evil."

All of this is significant when we focus on expressions of love on Valentine's Day. It is a time set aside where expressions of Love are to be shared and demonstrated. Most do this by sending a card, or giving Candy, or sending a Bouquet of Flowers. As a matter of fact, "The U.S. Greeting Card Association estimates that approximately one billion Valentines are sent each year world-wide." In many classrooms in our nation, younger children exchange cards with their teachers and friends. Basically, this is intended to be their expression of love. Most do not fully understand or appreciate the statements about Love but they share them just the same.

Love is more than an expression. It should be an overflow from the character and personality of one individual that affects and impacts another. It is an inner gift that utilizes words and deeds to demonstrate true feeling and emotion. Someone noted: "...in spite of all those cards that are exchanged, the Valentines that really matter are the ones we receive and give where love is unconditional, that say, No matter what- I love you!" One of the things that occurs in a pluralistic society is the blurring of the more meaningful gifts and allowing for something lesser as a substitute. For instance, George Barna recently conducted a Spiritual Gifts Survey and found the following: "...the latest study shows that just two-thirds of Christian Americans (68%) say they have heard of spiritual gifts..." The follow-up question asked which gifts the respondents believed they had.

"The most commonly claimed gifts were teaching (9%), service (8%) and faith (7%). Those were followed by encouragement (4%), healing (4%), knowledge (4%), tongues (3%), leadership (2%). The influence of the secular and pluralistic is seen in many of the respondents (21%) who deemed their Spiritual Gift to be: "a sense of humor, singing, health, life, happiness, patience, a job, a house, compromise, premonition, creativity, and clairvoyance." This is obviously a drift toward the subjective rather than an embrace of the objective.

The Word of God is very clear in its discussion of Spiritual Gifts and what they are: the passages of Scripture that teach about gifts include - Romans 12: 6-8, 1 Corinthians 12, Ephesians 4: 7-13, 1 Peter 4: 10-11. When it comes to Matters Of The Heart, I Corinthians 13:4-8 (NLT) is a passage that could and should be personalized by each of us:

- Love is patient and kind
- Love is not jealous or boastful or proud or rude.
- Love does not demand its own way.
- Love is not irritable, and it keeps no record of when it has been wronged.
- Love is never glad about injustice but rejoices whenever the truth wins out.

- Love never gives up, never loses faith, is always hopeful, and endures through every circumstance.
- Love will last forever…

It has been suggested that one insert his/her name where "Love" appears and the reading would be: "Jack/Jill is patient and kind; Jack/Jill is not jealous or boastful or proud or rude, Jack/Jill does not demand his/her own way, and so forth…

How much different life and relationships would be if we mutually embraced the words of Jesus recorded in John 13:34-35, "So now I am giving you a new commandment: Love each other. Just as I have loved you, you should love each other. Your love for one another will prove to the world that you are my disciples."

A secular song penned by Jackie DeShannon in 1965 reminded us from a secular viewpoint:

"What the world needs now is love, sweet love,
It's the only thing that there's just too little of…"

Let us be among those whose hearts overflow with love and compassion in our lives, families, communities, nation and world.

All of us are familiar with "Making A List"! There is the List of items needed from the store; things that need one's attention more immediately than not; bills that have to be paid; appointments that need to be kept; school assignments and test schedules; people who should be written or called; etc. When we approach Christmas-Time we are reminded in the song: "Santa Claus Is Coming To Town" – that – "he's making a list and checking it twice, he's gonna' find out whose been naughty or nice…"

Every year, Forbes publishes a list of the richest Americans. At the top of that list is Bill Gates of Microsoft, followed by Warren Buffet. Four of the Top Ten are Waltons who are heirs of the Wal-Mart empire. In terms of politics, C-Span developed a recent listing of the Top Best and Worst Presidents of the United States. Abraham Lincoln was ranked the best. George Washington was second, followed by Franklin D. Roosevelt, Theodore Roosevelt, Harry Truman and John F. Kennedy. Ronald Reagan was 10th. Bill Clinton was 15th. The survey graded each president on a scale of one ("not effective") to ten ("very effective"). The bottom five were: James Buchanan, Andrew Johnson, Franklin Pierce, William H. Harrison and Warren G. Harding. George W. Bush was 36th on the list. His dad was 18th. Such listings are subjective and will vary as time passes.

The United States Constitution is a statement regarding how this nation is to be governed. Attached to that Constitution are 27 Amendments that make stipulations and guarantee freedoms and rights. It makes this a land of law and order. "In the United States, the law is derived from four sources. These four sources are constitutional law, statutory law, administrative regulations, and the common law (which includes case law). The most important source of law is the United States Constitution. All other law falls under, and is subordinate to, that document. No law may contradict the Constitution. For example, if Congress enacts a statute that conflicts with the Constitution, the Supreme Court may find that law unconstitutional, and declare it invalid."

When we come to human behavior, we tend to relegate it to the Ethical norms. "Ethics refers to standards of behavior that tell us how human beings ought to act in the many situations in which they find themselves-as friends, parents, children, citizens, businesspeople, teachers, professionals, etc." Ethics is not the same as feelings. Feelings provide important information for our ethical choices. Ethics is not religion. Many people are not religious, but ethics applies to everyone. Most religions do advocate high ethical standards but sometimes do not address all the types of problems we face. Ethics is not following the law. A good system of law does incorporate many ethical standards, but law can deviate from what is ethical. Ethics is not following culturally accepted norms. Some cultures are quite ethical, but others become corrupt. Ethics is not science. Social and natural science can provide important data to help us make better ethical choices. But science alone does not tell us what we ought to do. Lists are endless. There seem to be Lists for everything. We have rules and regulations by the Bushel-Full. Long lists of "dos" and don'ts" become a blur.

God gave some very basic standards for life. The Ten Commandments were to govern (a) what people were to believe about God, and (b) what duties God was requiring of His people. In like manner, God gave man the Fruit of the Spirit that was to serve to develop positive Christian Behaviors for all of one's interactions. It fits within the framework of what Paul wrote Timothy - "Be an example for the believers in speech, in life, in love, in faith and in purity" (1 Timothy 4:12); and "Do your best to present yourself to God as a workman who is approved...who does not need be ashamed" (2 Timothy 2:15). Making a list and following it is NOT the desired goal, whereas making a Commitment to Christ and His Word IS the goal. Effectiveness in touching the lives of others will flow out from the level of Commitment one has made to the Lord Jesus Christ. Our Goal is to Know Him and to Make Him Known.

Remember Proverbs 4:23, "Keep your heart with all diligence, For out of it spring the issues of life." As we do so, we will please and honor Him!

CONSIDER THESE THINGS WITH ME!

Gumption and Unction

In the times in which we live, it is important to make the determination between "gumption" and "unction"! Our basic understanding of gumption is that it represents: "initiative; aggressiveness; resourcefulness; courage; spunk; guts; common sense; shrewdness." On the other hand, among the many definitions for unction, some of what it represents is: "that quality in language, address, or the like, which excites emotion; especially, strong devotion; religious fervor and tenderness; sometimes, a simulated, factitious, or unnatural fervor; smug self-serving earnestness; the application of a soothing or lubricating oil or ointment." As an aside, when reference is made to "soothing or lubricating oil or ointment, it brings to mind a recent advances in knee joint treatment. As an alternative to surgery, a treatment that is known considerable success is called Euflexxa Injection. "Euflexxa® is a highly purified hyaluronan, also called hyaluronic acid (HA) or sodium hyaluronate. HA is a natural substance found in the fluid that surrounds a healthy knee. This fluid is called synovial fluid and it helps cushion, lubricate, and protect the knee. In people with osteoarthritis (OA) of the knee, the synovial fluid becomes thinner and less able to do its job. Euflexxa® is similar to the HA found in healthy knees. When Euflexxa® is injected into the knee, it replenishes the HA in the knee and helps restore the ability of the synovial fluid to cushion, lubricate, and protect the knee. Euflexxa® is different from pills because it works right at the source of pain and is not distributed throughout your body."

However, in coming back to the use of words, they are what they are – promises with no clinical substantiation. There is no immediate physical benefit to the spoken word that is not followed through with action and benefit. If one is giving a speech in a secular arena, one should remember that it is action that will speak louder than any spoken word. It is the intent of what is recorded in James 2:14-18 (NKJV), "What does it profit, my brethren, if someone says he has faith but does not have works? Can faith save him? If a brother or sister is naked and destitute of daily food, and one of you says to them, Depart in peace, be warmed and filled, but you do not give them the things which are needed for the body, what does it profit? Thus also faith by itself, if it does not have works, is dead. But someone will say, You have faith, and I have works. Show me your faith without your works, and I will show you my faith by my works." The Message paraphrase is very direct in its rendering of these verses: "Dear friends, do you think you'll get anywhere in this if you learn all the right words but never do anything? Does merely talking about faith indicate that a person really has it? For instance, you come upon an old friend dressed in rags and half-starved and say, Good morning, friend! Be clothed in Christ! Be filled with the Holy Spirit! and walk off without providing so much as a coat or a cup of soup - where does that get you? Isn't it obvious that God-talk without God-acts is outrageous nonsense? I can already hear one of you agreeing by saying, Sounds good. You take care of the faith department, I'll handle the works department. Not so fast. You can no more show me your works apart from your faith than I can show you my faith apart from my works. Faith and works, works and faith, fit together hand in glove."

  Within the lifetime of many of us, we have been exposed to and had the experience of listening to gifted orators who have uttered memorable lines that are easily quoted: John F. Kennedy - "Ask not what your country can do for you – Ask what you can do for your country!" Then the memorable lines from (Martin Luther King): "I have a dream..." The election of 2008 may have been determined because of a gifted orator and his oratory. The promise of "change" and the encouragement that "we" can bring it about. In retrospect, a valid question should have been: At what cost will this change be brought about? Big and costly Government has come in with a roar and the majority has voted for great and increasing expenditures. The Congressional Budget Office (Non-Partisan) has warned: "The...stimulus package proposed will actually hurt the economy more in the long run than if we did absolutely nothing...The bill would help create small economic stimulation in the short term, but our government will be up to its eyeballs in debt that within a few years it would crowd out private investment. What happens when this occurs? Well, this will lead to a lower GDP (Gross Domestic Product) over the next 10 years. We are talking between a 0.1 and 0.3 reduction in GDP." Rhetoric can move people to consensus and hope – Arithmetic should shock people into reality and apprehension.

When one thinks in a religious context, gumption and unction are equally important. Gumption would focus upon the commitment of an individual to the cause and/or calling. Unction has other ramifications. In addition to extreme unction that is part of the ministry of one large world-wide Church, there is an application to the spoken word in a religious ceremony or service, namely, that unction represents: "God's unmistakable presence attending and empowering the preaching of His Truth... unction is commonly referred to as the anointing of the Holy Spirit. Preaching with unction occurs because of the anointing of the Holy Spirit." This type of preaching is typical in a Biblical context as the moment when Elijah challenged the prophets of Baal on Mount Carmel (I Kings 18), or when Peter preached on the Day of Pentecost (Acts 2). In modern day religious services, there is very little demonstration of "unction" and far too much function instead. It leaves one wondering whether or not one can function in the junction if there is continuance on that road.

The narrow focus of unction is stated in the following: "Unction is the result of careful and diligent preparation, having earnestly sought God in prayer for Him to do what He wills to do with the preparation that has gone forth. Careful and diligent preparation concerns both the messenger as well as the message to be preached. Certainly the preacher must spend time in personal reflection, prayer, confession and personal commitment regarding the truth he has discovered. Unless he has made himself the initial audience of the sermon that he will ultimately preach to others, he will not preach with unction. This is the subjective preparation needed in order to preach effectively."

Edward M. Bounds wrote many tomes on Prayer and the need for a basic relationship with the Triune God. In Power Through Prayer, he has a chapter called: "Unction A Necessity." It begins with a statement by Charles Haddon Spurgeon in which he states: "One bright benison (blessing, benediction) which private prayer brings down upon the ministry is an indescribable and inimitable something -- an unction from the Holy One... If the anointing which we bear comes not from the Lord of hosts, we are deceivers, since only in prayer can we obtain it. Let us continue instant constant fervent in supplication. Let your fleece lie on the thrashing floor of supplication till it is wet with the dew of heaven."

E, M. Bounds also quotes Alexander Knox, a Christian philosopher of the days of Wesley said..."The clergy, too generally have absolutely lost the art. There is, I conceive, in the great laws of the moral world a kind of secret understanding like the affinities in chemistry, between rightly promulgated religious truth and the deepest feelings of the human mind. Where the one is duly exhibited, the other will respond. Did not our hearts burn within us? -- but to this devout feeling is indispensable in the speaker. Now, I am obliged to state from my own observation that this unction, as the French not unfitly term it, is beyond all comparison more likely to be found in England in a Methodist conventicle (a secret or unauthorized meeting, esp. for religious worship) than in a parish Church. This, and this alone, seems really to be that which fills the Methodist houses and thins the Churches...This unction is the art of preaching. The preacher who never had this unction never had the art of preaching. The preacher who has lost this unction has lost the art of preaching. Whatever other arts he may have and retain -- the art of sermon-making, the art of eloquence, the art of great, clear thinking, the art of pleasing an audience -- he has lost the divine art of preaching. This unction makes God's truth powerful and interesting, draws and attracts, edifies, convicts, saves. This unction vitalizes God's revealed truth, makes it living and life-giving. Even God's truth spoken without this unction is light, dead, and deadening…

Mr. Spurgeon says: "I wonder how long we might beat our brains before we could plainly put into word what is meant by preaching with unction. Yet he who preaches knows its presence, and he who hears soon detects its absence…Such is the mystery of spiritual anointing. We know, but we cannot tell to others what it is. It is as easy as it is foolish, to counterfeit it. Unction is a thing which you cannot manufacture, and its counterfeits are worse than worthless. Yet it is, in itself, priceless, and beyond measure needful if you would edify believers and bring sinners to Christ."

Those are powerful words for consideration by the follower of Christ in particular, as well as the Church in general. There seems to be a growing need in the hearts and minds of people everywhere. There's an inner itch that needs to be scratched. The spiritual search for many has been interrupted and almost brought to a stop. The secular quest is frustrated by an absent stability in the marketplace. The plight of investors has been a negative experience and funds set aside for retirement have been reduced by almost fifty percent because of the unscrupulous activity of greedy and unconscionable people. The plans and hopes for ones future have been dashed – dashed because of pernicious acts (causing insidious harm or ruin) by unethical, immoral and greedy people. One reason why this could so easily occur is the innocence of people – people who deemed others to be trustworthy and in whom they had confidence. They realized too late that they had been duped and that they were both gullible and naïve to the ways of the investment world. We have all heard of wolves in sheep's clothing – well those who were trusted with peoples funds proved to be thieves in business suits.

Our nation has been too easily influenced by outstanding oratory and rhetoric. The downside to be influenced in such a way is that it allows one to become gullible and less rationale. In listening to various media personalities and preachers, it is amazing to observe how often the target is missed and diatribe takes up the time. The bottom line to all of this is that it becomes an issue of content – (a) the content of a man's character and commitment; and (b) the content and conviction attached to what that man says. The basic pedagogic purpose is missing. At the end of the day, the goal is: This is what you need to know, to think, and to do – now! Anything other than that becomes voluminous vicissitudes (change or variation occurring in the course of something).

In a drastically uncertain and changing world, Peter addressed the Church and believers who were being scattered and killed because of the persecution by Roman Rulers. Peter emphasized that even in the worst case scenario the Believer had an obligation to both live and act correctly within a decadent and harsh culture. His words are in II Peter 1:2-11 (NKJV):

"Grace and peace be multiplied to you in the knowledge of God and of Jesus our Lord, as His divine power has given to us all things that pertain to life and godliness, through the knowledge of Him who called us by glory and virtue, by which have been given to us exceedingly great and precious promises, that through these you may be partakers of the divine nature, having escaped the corruption that is in the world through lust. But also for this very reason, giving all diligence, add to your faith virtue, to virtue knowledge, to knowledge self-control, to self-control perseverance, to perseverance godliness, to godliness brotherly kindness, and to brotherly kindness love. For if these things are yours and abound, you will be neither barren nor unfruitful in the knowledge of our Lord Jesus Christ. For he who lacks these things is shortsighted, even to blindness, and has forgotten that he was cleansed from his old sins. Therefore, brethren, be even more diligent to make your call and election sure, for if you do these things you will never stumble; for so an entrance will be supplied to you abundantly into the everlasting kingdom of our Lord and Savior Jesus Christ."

The words shared by Peter are powerful. Note just a few:

His divine power has granted to us all things that pertain to life and godliness, through the knowledge of him who called us to his own glory and excellence, by which he has granted to us his precious and very great promises, so that through them you may become partakers of the divine nature, having escaped from the corruption that is in the world because of sinful desire…"

- His Divine Power has granted us all things…
- His Precious and Very Great Promises…
- Become partakers of the Divine Nature

"…be all the more diligent to make your calling and election sure, for if you practice these qualities you will never fall…"

What are "these qualities"? "…supplement your faith

- with virtue
- with knowledge
- with self-control
- with steadfastness
- with godliness
- with brotherly affection
- with love.

"For if these qualities are yours and are increasing, they keep you from being ineffective or unfruitful in the knowledge of our Lord Jesus Christ."

- ✓ These qualities must be increasing
- ✓ They will keep you from being ineffective
- ✓ They will keep you from being unfruitful

Peter was indicating that these things needed to be the life-choice and life-commitment for each believer. These are the foundational principles and core values for the obedient Christian.

The difficult circumstances of life should never alter, affect or negatively impact the one who has become a partaker of the Divine Nature. The virtues and qualities spoken of by Peter should be increasing – even during times of adversity.

If you had been alive in Peter's day, how would you have responded to his writing and teaching? Would you have thought there was important merit to his communication? Would you have renewed your commitment to follow Jesus Christ – even if it meant all the way to Calvary?

He bottom-line is – it's not what you say – it's what you do! It's not just the talk – it's what's proven by your walk!

CONSIDER THESE THINGS WITH ME!

Myrmidons

Do you fear the coming of the Myrmidons? Are they aliens from outer space? Is it a germ that will become pandemic? Is there an inoculation to prevent any contagion caused by a Myrmidon? Should the exterminator be called to see what he can do to contain the progress of the Myrmidon? Is it like a bedbug or something similar to it? Or, is The Myrmidon – not a contagion but a secular and political movement?

One can look at our world, or our nation, and muse whether or not government and rule has become the rule and government by Myrmidons (a faithful follower who carries out orders without question; a person who executes without question or scruple a master's commands; A member of a warlike Thessalian people who were ruled by Achilles and followed him on the expedition against Troy).

Historically, we have seen it during World War II and the rise and power of Nazism. We get a sense of this type of commitment from the representations about the Taliban, Al Qaeda and Radical Islam. It appears we have arrived at a similar place where the nation has become euphoric about the possibilities of change to the point of almost a lock-step (or goose-step march) approach to government by the elected partisans.

In the Stimulus Package that was presented in 2008 and 2009 and voted upon – no one had time to read or study it. It was classified as an emergency and presented so that it had to be enacted if catastrophe was to be averted. The result was the blind passage of the Stimulus Package along Party lines (with the exception of three Republican Senators). There has been a political advertisement that suggests the following: If from the time of the Birth of Jesus Christ there was the expenditure of $1,000,000.00 per day up to today, it would not total or equal the amount of the planned Stimulus infusion of cash based upon the passage of the Stimulus Package. Emboldened by the Congressional approval, there is now the presentation of a 4 Billion Dollar Budget. The Hill has published an editorial by Dick Morris (February 24, 2009) in which he states: "There are bad loans, which became bad assets, that lie at the root of the crisis. Through deregulation by the government and the greed of financial institutions, they spread to every portfolio in the world. But these basic facts have metastasized out of all proportion to their real harm into job and financial insecurity for every family on Earth...Previous panics have been global in impact, but local in focus. The world panicked because of developments in Mexico or Argentina or Thailand or South Korea. Now, with Collateralized Debt Obligations spreading the poison of a bunch of bad loans all over the world, infecting every portfolio, the panic is not only global in impact but in focus as well. Modern communications have hastened the spread of the virus of panic throughout the global bloodstream."

In a Christian Post article (February 25, 2009) the following is noted: "Though a large portion of Americans are cutting back on donations to non-profits amid tough economic conditions, evangelical parachurch ministries have been among those least affected by the cuts...According to the survey by the Evangelical Council for Financial Accountability (ECFA), most evangelical parachurch ministries exceeded, met or came very close to their 2008 fourth-quarter contributions goals. Many of the parachurch ministries we surveyed reported small donations of $10 to $100 were relatively unaffected, and in some cases, donations in this category increased...In fact, some of our members had the strongest fourth quarter they've had in years and ended the year debt-free. In a survey of ECFA members, 72 percent of responding organizations reportedly exceeded, met or came within 10 percent of their goals. The remaining 28 percent said they were more than 10 percent below their goals.

The ECFA also noted: "The opportunities to help those in financial need are greater than organizations can supply... but I believe that Christians are stepping up and being perhaps even more generous at this time when they consider the great need of people today."

There is a very meaningful passage in the Holy Scriptures that speaks of the will and determination of a people to step up and sacrifice in order to help meet the needs in the Church and World. It is II Corinthians 8:1-5 (ESV), "We want you to know…about the grace of God that has been given among the churches of Macedonia, for in a severe test of affliction, their abundance of joy and their extreme poverty have overflowed in a wealth of generosity on their part. For they gave according to their means, as I can testify, and beyond their means, of their own accord, begging us earnestly for the favor of taking part in the relief of the saints - and this, not as we expected, but they gave themselves first to the Lord and then by the will of God to us." What a tremendous approach and attitude by those who had so little. They "begged" for the opportunity to give and to share what they had with those who had less.

Paul summarizes his thoughts and instructions about giving in II Corinthians 9:6-11 (ESV), "The point is this: whoever sows sparingly will also reap sparingly, and whoever sows bountifully will also reap bountifully. Each one must give as he has decided in his heart, not reluctantly or under compulsion, for God loves a cheerful giver. And God is able to make all grace abound to you, so that having all sufficiency in all things at all times, you may abound in every good work. As it is written, He has distributed freely, he has given to the poor; his righteousness endures forever. He who supplies seed to the sower and bread for food will supply and multiply your seed for sowing and increase the harvest of your righteousness. You will be enriched in every way to be generous in every way, which through us will produce thanksgiving to God." The promise is that God will continue to take care of His faithful people.

The following passage is referenced frequently and the hope is that it will not become hackneyed in our thinking. The bottom-line for the Church and Professing Christian is the implementation of James 2:14-18 (NLT), "Dear brothers and sisters, what's the use of saying you have faith if you don't prove it by your actions? That kind of faith can't save anyone. Suppose you see a brother or sister who needs food or clothing, and you say, Well, good-bye and God bless you; stay warm and eat well – but then you don't give that person any food or clothing. What good does that do? So it isn't enough just to have faith. Faith that doesn't show itself by good deeds is no faith at all – it is dead and useless…"

In our day and time, these passages should be our ongoing concern and sensitivity. The need is great but the ability of our God to provide for and through us is far greater. We are to be good stewards of that which the Lord has entrusted to us. We don't want to err by becoming insensitive or stingy in our approach to the needs current in our time. Caring and Sharing is always a good approach to meeting the genuine needs of those who are less fortunate or who have fallen on hard times. Don't be one who passes by on the other side when a need is observed or made known. In a very restricted sense, you can be a Myrmidon – "a faithful follower who carries out orders without question"! Biblically, giving to needs of others is always voluntary, but giving is always a mark of obedience to a caring God.

CONSIDER THESE THINGS WITH ME!

Forms of Filicide

To indicate that our nation is living in changing and strange times is an understatement. What is occurring is something more than just a mere transition. If our nation shifts from being Capitalist to Socialist – that is a major revamping of the very foundations upon which we were founded. Additionally, if we somehow lose our moral compass and conscience as a nation, we will become directionless and susceptible to new behaviors that are borne out of a personal rationale that has freed itself from either ethical or moral values and standards. We are beginning to see sad evidences and consequences of these behaviors.

On February 12, 2009 - we were confronted and shocked by the headline that read: "Bridges TV Founder Charged with Wife's Beheading"! This did not occur in some other country where beheading is a so-called "religious practice." This occurred in Buffalo, NY at a radio station. Sadly, it leaves two children aged four and six deprived of their Mother and separated from their imprisoned Father. Also, we read and hear all too frequently about missing children and their subsequent deaths. A lurking question pertains to whether or not "filicide" lurks in the psyche of a growing number of people within our culture.

Why is filicide occurring today? Have people lost their way? Do they no longer have any hope? Have they become detached from spiritual alternatives and resolve? Has their desperateness short-circuited their logic and reason?

FILICIDE is not historically new. It is the deliberate act of a parent killing his or her own son or daughter. The word filicide derives from the Latin word "filius" meaning "son". In some cultures, killing a daughter who is deemed to have disgraced the family is a common occurrence (see honor killing). A 1999 US Department of Justice Study concluded that between 1976 and 1997 in the United States, mothers were responsible for a higher share of children killed during infancy while fathers were more likely to have been responsible for the murders of children age 8 or older. Furthermore, 52% of the children killed by their mothers were male (maternal filicide), while 57% of the children killed by their fathers were male (paternal filicide).

Sometimes there is a combination of murder and suicide in filicide cases. There are some historical examples of Filicide:

- Ptolemy XII of Egypt had his daughter Berenice IV and her husband beheaded in 55 BC. This was after she had dethroned him and poisoned her sister, Cleopatra VI.
- Ivan IV of Russia (Ivan the Terrible) killed his son and heir to the throne in a fit of rage.
- Peter the Great of Russia had his son tortured to death, being present at several of the torture sessions and allegedly participating in some of them.
- Josef and Magda Goebbels poisoned their six children, in order to protect them from the invading Soviet Army, before committing suicide.
- Motown singer-songwriter Marvin Gaye was shot to death by his father on April 1, 1984.
- Professional wrestler Chris Benoit killed his seven year old son Daniel, along with his wife and himself, on June 23, 2007.

We also forget the example of Forms of Filicide in the Bible – (a) Cain killing his brother Abel; (b) the sacrificing of children to Molech in the fire (Leviticus 20:1-5). The force of the Lord's intent is summarized in Leviticus 18:21, "Do not give any of your children to be sacrificed to Molech, for you must not profane the name of your God. I am the Lord."

In addition to filicide, we also have fratricide "a person who kills his or her brother" (the case of Cain killing his brother Abel). We also have genocide – "the deliberate and systematic extermination of a national, racial, political, or cultural group" (like Hitler doing Ethnic Cleansing during World War II). One other instance where the sanctity of life has eroded is when a person can no longer face the personal responsibilities and obligations of life. The only alternative or option that they see is suicide – "a person who intentionally takes his or her own life." The most gross form of causing the death of another is by Abortion. It is called aborticide or feticide – "the removal of an embryo or fetus from the uterus in order to end a pregnancy."

When we consider these different categories of terminating a life, we must consider what role, if any, we have to reach out to the desperate individuals whose only conceived escape is the termination of a human life.

The words of Proverbs 24:10-12 are very sobering – "If you faint in the day of adversity, your strength is small. Rescue those who are being taken away to death; hold back those who are stumbling to the slaughter. If you say, Behold, we did not know this, does not he who weighs the heart perceive it? Does not he who keeps watch over your soul know it, and will he not repay man according to his work?" We have a duty toward the weak, hurting and stumbling souls in this world. We should be more attuned to preventative intervention in the lives of the troubled and desperate.

These verses in The Message state: "If you fall to pieces in a crisis, there wasn't much to you in the first place. Rescue the perishing; don't hesitate to step in and help. If you say, "Hey, that's none of my business," will that get you off the hook? Someone is watching you closely, you know - Someone not impressed with weak excuses."

In case you were wondering, the New Living Translation states these verses this way: "If you fail under pressure, your strength is not very great. Rescue those who are unjustly sentenced to death; don't stand back and let them die. Don't try to avoid responsibility by saying you didn't know about it. For God knows all hearts, and he sees you. He keeps watch over your soul, and he knows you knew! And he will judge all people according to what they have done."

Another aspect to this subject is the very beautiful words about life and the full and fulfilled dimension of it in Psalm 139:14-18 – "I praise you, for I am fearfully and wonderfully made. Wonderful are your works; my soul knows it very well. My frame was not hidden from you, when I was being made in secret, intricately woven in the depths of the earth. Your eyes saw my unformed substance; in your book were written, every one of them, the days that were formed for me, when as yet there was none of them. How precious to me are your thoughts, O God! How vast is the sum of them! If I would count them, they are more than the sand. I awake, and I am still with you."

It is obvious that we need to return to our moral base and core values. In the midst of changing and difficult times, the compassionate Lord's invitation remains as the clarion call to the troubled in heart, or soul, or mind – Matthew 11:28-30 where Jesus said: "Come to me, all you who are weary and burdened - I will give you rest. Take my yoke upon you and learn from me, for I am gentle and humble in heart, and you will find rest for your souls. For my yoke is easy and my burden is light." Rest for your soul! These words resonate for the confused, disenfranchised, uncertain, directionless, weary and oppressed. Just come!

Seek the Lord while He may be found, call upon Him while He is near! Just come!

Implement Proverbs 3:5-6 (The Message): "Trust God from the bottom of your heart; don't try to figure out everything on your own. Listen for God's voice in everything you do, everywhere you go; He's the one who will keep you on track." Just come!

You'll be glad you came to Him!

CONSIDER THESE THINGS WITH ME!

Enfilading

There is an increasing frequency of Truth being sacrificed on the Altar of political correctness and convenience. Those who serve their country during wartime and in battle areas know what it is to be subjected to an enemy who is relentless in enfilading. When a command is given: "Ready! Aim! Fire!" the troops respond with an enfilade. It is: "A firing in the direction of the length of a trench, or a line of parapet or troops, etc.; a raking fire; to pierce, scour, or rake with shot in the direction of the length of, as a work, or a line of troops." Most have heard of the Gatlin Gun. It was first used in the Civil War by the Union Forces. The man who invented it – Dr. Richard J. Gatlin – wrote that he made it "…to reduce the size of armies and so cut down on the number of deaths by combat and disease." That rationale has led to more sophisticated weaponry of modern warfare to the point where great numbers of people can be vaporized by nuclear weapons and combat soldiers can be wounded or die by the use of a variety armor piercing devices.

In the area of political debate, enfilading is a device and method used in terms of verbal attack where the desire is to marginalized a political opponent by either misquoting or by means of ridicule. Reference was made to this approach in a post submitted on the subject of "kerfuffling"! One who is said to kerfuffle means to be part of: "a disorderly outburst or tumult; a commotion." Accuracy and Truth are no longer championed. A statement is lifted out of context: "I want President Obama to fail…", spoken by Rush Limbaugh, and the enfilading begins. Context is ignored and enfilading begins. The context of what Rush Limbaugh said was: "I want Barack Obama to fail if his mission is to restructure and reform this country so that capitalism and individual liberty are not its foundation? Why would I want that to succeed?" Context makes quite a difference. An old saying is: "A text taken out of its context is a pretext." That is a truism all too often in political discourse.

What gets lost in the immediate is that in 2008 51% of Democrats polled wanted President Bush to fail, and almost as many indicated that General Patraeus would lie to Congressional Committees about the War in Iraq. Why? Because they were not interested in the facts delivered by the Field General in charge of the Surge in Iraq, but in their presupposition that the War was already lost. And so, Posters were circulated about a General who was serving his country that read: "Not General Patraeus but General Betray-Us"! It not only sets out to marginalize, but also includes destruction of reputation, personal integrity, and the brilliant strategy and accomplishment of a career officer. In this instance, they failed! However, those given to enfilading are versatile and opportunistic. They shift their guns from Bush and Cheney to other targets and a different debate. It had Rush Limbaugh being portrayed as the "head of the Republican Party" even though he has never run for political office, nor has he sought to do so. What must be remembered here is a more subtle strategy. Since the new administration has assumed responsibility for the nation, members of Congress have raised the issue regarding The Fairness Doctrine - "The policy of the United States Federal Communications Commission that became known as the Fairness Doctrine is an attempt to ensure that all coverage of controversial issues by a broadcast station be balanced and fair. The FCC took the view in 1949, that station licensees were public trustees, and as such had an obligation to afford reasonable opportunity for discussion of contrasting points of view on controversial issues of public importance..." The lament has been that the airwaves are saturated with Conservative Talk Show Hosts, and there are few, if any, comparable Liberal Talk Shows on Radio. It cannot be denied that effort was made to have an entire network devoted to a Liberal Point of View. The problem – there was no audience committed to that network or such programming.

Enfilading

There is usually a "mob Mentality" lurking and waiting for an opportune moment to spew forth the pent up venom. It is usually a core of liberal thinkers. Whether it is a political position or one that is religious, the liberal will be ready to attack and put the more conservative movement, cause, or person in the spotlight of misquotes and disinformation – all those who represent the Truth will be subjected to verbal enfilading and be both marginalized and/or ridiculed along the way.

Just look at the life of Jesus Christ and the accusations that were directed at Him. In Luke 5:29-33, "Levi made him a great feast in his house, and there was a large company of tax collectors and others reclining at table with them. And the Pharisees and their scribes grumbled at his disciples, saying, Why do you eat and drink with tax collectors and sinners? And Jesus answered them, Those who are well have no need of a physician, but those who are sick. I have not come to call the righteous but sinners to repentance. And they said to him, The disciples of John fast often and offer prayers, and so do the disciples of the Pharisees, but yours eat and drink." What was being attempted here by the Pharisees? What was their long-term goal, as well as their immediate objective? Obviously, it was their attempt to discredit Jesus and marginalize His ministry. An interesting statement was made in a random Blog about Marginalization. In part, it stated the following opinion: "We live in a postmodern, pluralistic culture and relish the idea that we are the most religiously diverse society in the world. Every religion is correct and no one has the right to say anyone else's faith is wrong. Political correctness demands great care in the use of terminology when referring to deity; gender neutrality and inclusiveness are essential; exclusiveness is to be rejected.

"Postmodernism involves, among other things, the denial of absolutes. What constitutes "truth" is determined by each individual's personal experience. Thus, truth becomes entirely relative; what is true for "you" may not necessarily be true for "me." Pluralism is a concept which supposedly accepts every religion as equally valid. There is, however, one exception: Christianity. Christianity is not tolerated by those who boast of their "toleration" because of its exclusivity. Unacceptable in a postmodern society, ever increasing pressure to is being brought to bear to marginalize Christianity in the Western world. And in an ever increasing number of Eastern countries laws are being enacted outlawing "conversion activities" of any kind by Christians."

The writer of the preceding is very close to the bulls-eye. The task of serving Christ is daunting and the road may lead one "through the valley of the shadow of death", but at such times and in such places one must continually remember – even there – The Lord Continues To Be My Shepherd – and because He is, I have everything that I need and I can endure everything for Him!

The prelude to the great Faith Chapter – Hebrews 11 – makes important points in terms of the assurance of faith. How does one secure faith? How does one maintain faith? Note what is said in Hebrews 10 :22-25.

- Let us draw near with a true heart in full assurance of faith, with our hearts sprinkled clean from an evil conscience and our bodies washed with pure water
- Let us hold fast the confession of our hope without wavering, for he who promised is faithful.
- Let us consider how to stir up one another to love and good works,
- Let us not neglect meeting together, as is the habit of some,
- Let us encourage one another, and all the more as you see the Day drawing near.

These are important principles and ingredients if one is to be a person of faith, integrity and commitment.

In Hebrews 10:35-39, we read these important words:

Enfilading

"...do not throw away your confidence, which has a great reward. For you have need of endurance, so that when you have done the will of God you may receive what is promised. For, Yet a little while, and the coming one will come and will not delay; but my righteous one shall live by faith, and if he shrinks back, my soul has no pleasure in him. But we are not of those who shrink back and are destroyed, but of those who have faith and preserve their souls.

The important thrust and the word that should impact each of us is: "we are not of those who shrink back and are destroyed, but of those who have faith and preserve their souls." Regardless of the enfilading that may occur and be directed at anyone of us "...we are not of those who shrink back...but of those who have faith and preserve their souls." Regardless if one is persecuted and/or falsely accused, "we are not of those who shrink back...but of those who have faith and preserve their souls." Even though attempts may be made to silence the words we speak and the message we proclaim, "...we are not of those who shrink back...but of those who have faith and preserve their souls."

Near the end of Hebrews 11, there is a statement made regarding the extent of suffering and persecution. They are stirring words in Hebrews 11:32-38, "And what more shall I say? For time would fail me to tell of Gideon, Barak, Samson, Jephthah, of David and Samuel and the prophets - who through faith conquered kingdoms, enforced justice, obtained promises, stopped the mouths of lions, quenched the power of fire, escaped the edge of the sword, were made strong out of weakness, became mighty in war, put foreign armies to flight...Some were tortured, refusing to accept release, so that they might rise again to a better life. Others suffered mocking and flogging, and even chains and imprisonment. They were stoned, they were sawn in two, they were killed with the sword. They went about in skins of sheep and goats, destitute, afflicted, mistreated - of whom the world was not worthy - wandering about in deserts and mountains, and in dens and caves of the earth..."

At the end of the day, even though the forces of evil thought they had triumphed over the righteous and righteousness, the epitaph is clear and precise, namely, "of whom the world was not worthy."

The one who follows Christ has a tremendous heritage. It is summarized in I Corinthians 15:57-58, "But thanks be to God, who gives us the victory through our Lord Jesus Christ. Therefore, my beloved brothers, be steadfast, immovable, always abounding in the work of the Lord, knowing that in the Lord your labor is not in vain.

The same summary in The Message Paraphrase is: "But now in a single victorious stroke of Life, all three - sin, guilt, death - are gone, the gift of our Master, Jesus Christ. Thank God! With all this going for us, my dear, dear friends, stand your ground. And don't hold back. Throw yourselves into the work of the Master, confident that nothing you do for him is a waste of time or effort."

This is our legacy and heritage. Serve the Lord with gladness, courage, confidence and victoriously.

CONSIDER THESE THINGS WITH ME!

Foundational Dysfunction?

For quite a while, we have been subjected to the hew and cry regarding the separation of Church and State. It surfaces regularly regarding the celebration of Easter or Christmas, or whenever a public religious display or expression is forthcoming. While the Pledge of Allegiance still retains the words, "one nation, under God", and while our coins and currency continue to indicate, "In God We Trust", nevertheless there is an ongoing effort to eliminate any reference to God or Christ – in public – in our nation.

Michael Spencer is a writer and communicator. He has recently written: "The Coming Evangelical Collapse", in which he states: "Evangelicalism needs a 'rescue mission' from the world Christian community… Some will continue to see conservatism and Christianity through one lens and will engage the culture war much as before – a status quo the media will be all too happy to perpetuate. A significant number, however, may give up political engagement for a discipleship of deeper impact. Is all of this a bad thing? Evangelicalism doesn't need a bailout. Much of it needs a funeral. But what about what remains? Is it a good thing that denominations are going to become largely irrelevant? Only if the networks that replace them are able to marshal resources, training, and vision to the mission field and into the planting and equipping of churches. Is it a good thing that many marginal believers will depart? Possibly, if churches begin and continue the work of renewing serious church membership. We must change the conversation from the maintenance of traditional churches to developing new and culturally appropriate ones.."

Michael Spencer continues: "…Will the coming collapse get Evangelicals past the pragmatism and shallowness that has brought about the loss of substance and power? Probably not. The purveyors of the evangelical circus will be in fine form, selling their wares as the promised solution to every church's problems. I expect the landscape of mega-church vacuity to be around for a very long time. Will it shake lose the prosperity Gospel from its parasitical place on the evangelical body of Christ? Evidence from similar periods is not encouraging. American Christians seldom seem to be able to separate their theology from an overall idea of personal affluence and success...We can rejoice that in the ruins, new forms of Christian vitality and ministry will be born. I expect to see a vital and growing house church movement. This cannot help but be good for an evangelicalism that has made buildings, numbers, and paid staff its drugs for half a century. We need new evangelicalism that learns from the past and listens more carefully to what God says about being His people in the midst of a powerful, idolatrous culture..."

The concept regarding Culture Wars was reintroduced in the 1991 publication - Culture Wars: The Struggle to Define America by James Davison Hunter...In it, Hunter described what he saw as a dramatic realignment and polarization that had transformed American Politics and Culture. He argued that on an increasing number of...defining issues – abortion...separation of church and state, privacy, recreational drug use, homosexuality, and censorship issues – has led to two definable polarities...Hunter characterized this polarity as stemming from opposite impulses, toward what he refers to as Progressivism and Orthodoxy.

In 1992, Patrick Buchanan became a Republican candidate for President. In his Convention speech, he said: "There is a religious war going on in our country for the soul of America. It is a cultural war, as critical to the kind of nation we will one day be as was the Cold War itself." In addition to criticizing "environmental extremists" and "radical feminism," he said, "...public morality has become a defining issue." Buchanan elaborated that this conflict was about power over society's definition of right and wrong. He named abortion, sexual orientation and popular culture as major fronts – and mentioned other controversies, including clashes over "Christmas Observance, Nativity Scenes in

Foundational Dysfunction?

Public Places, Taxpayer funded art (some very obscene), and discrimination against religious schools…"

On The Culture War Website, part of the Introductory Comments are: "For the past 150 years new ideas and discoveries in science have challenged the traditional Christian World View, that God created the Earth, Sun, Moon, the stars and all life on Earth. Dr. D. James Kennedy has said, "The Cultural War is a difference in the World Viewpoints between believers and non-believers of Christ."

The Cultural War has been formed and defined by a number of discovers and new theories that were developed in the 19th and 20th centuries, that have molded the present day mind set of American Society. New discoveries in the past ten years are casting some doubt on theories of the past two centuries. While some are eager to latch onto the new ideas, many others are still holding onto the old ideas and values of the past. A recent national poll that asked, "Do you believe there is a God?" Eighty five percent of Americans who answered the question, said "Yes" they do believe in a supreme being, which becomes a central world view defining the Culture War in America."

There are basic eternal truths that should not be ignored as Spencer's thoughts are pondered and ruminated. The first truth pertains to what Jesus taught regarding the wheat and the weeds – Matthew 13:24-30, "The kingdom of heaven may be compared to a man who sowed good seed in his field, but while his men were sleeping, his enemy came and sowed weeds among the wheat and went away. So when the plants came up and bore grain, then the weeds appeared also. And the servants of the master of the house came and said to him, Master, did you not sow good seed in your field? How then does it have weeds? He said to them, An enemy has done this. So the servants said to him, Then do you want us to go and gather them? But he said, No, lest in gathering the weeds you root up the wheat along with them. Let both grow together until the harvest, and at harvest time I will tell the reapers, Gather the weeds first and bind them in bundles to be burned, but gather the wheat into my barn. The second truth pertains to the Lord's declaration in Matthew 16:18, "...I will build my church, and the gates of hell shall not prevail against it..."

The Lord has an eternal plan – but - we can only see parts of it gradually unfolding. It should not cause one any panic or undue fear because the Lord has determined a precise time and an exact moment when all of the absurdity and confusion of mankind will arrive at His Termination Point. Until then, in the ebb and flow of Christianity (so-called), one will realize disappointments and disillusionment.

There are words of caution and warning given to the Seven Churches in Revelation 2 and 3. There is a clear and definitive statement made to each Church regarding the intrusion of the culture into the church. Just an illustration or two will suffice: (Revelation 2:12-17), "And to the angel of the church in Pergamum write: The words of him who has the sharp two-edged sword. I know where you dwell, where Satan's throne is. Yet you hold fast my name, and you did not deny my faith even in the days of Antipas my faithful witness, who was killed among you, where Satan dwells. But I have a few things against you: you have some there who hold the teaching of Balaam, who taught Balak to put a stumbling block before the sons of Israel, so that they might eat food sacrificed to idols and practice sexual immorality. So also you have some who hold the teaching of the Nicolaitans. Therefore repent. If not, I will come to you soon and war against them with the sword of my mouth. He who has an ear, let him hear what the Spirit says to the churches. To the one who conquers I will give some of the hidden manna, and I will give him a white stone, with a new name written on the stone that no one knows except the one who receives it." Clearly, this Church had been infiltrated by the Secularists of that day, and had succumbed to the influences of the permissive religious culture – all in the name of peace at any cost and tolerance.

The subtlety of the culture war can be seen in the second illustration (Revelation 3:14-22): "And to the angel of the church

Foundational Dysfunction?

in Laodicea write: The words of the Amen, the faithful and true witness, the beginning of God's creation. I know your works: you are neither cold nor hot. Would that you were either cold or hot! So, because you are lukewarm, and neither hot nor cold, I will spit you out of my mouth. For you say, I am rich, I have prospered, and I need nothing, not realizing that you are wretched, pitiable, poor, blind, and naked. I counsel you to buy from me gold refined by fire, so that you may be rich, and white garments so that you may clothe yourself and the shame of your nakedness may not be seen, and salve to anoint your eyes, so that you may see. Those whom I love, I reprove and discipline, so be zealous and repent. Behold, I stand at the door and knock. If anyone hears my voice and opens the door, I will come in to him and eat with him, and he with me. The one who conquers, I will grant him to sit with me on my throne, as I also conquered and sat down with my Father on his throne. He who has an ear, let him hear what the Spirit says to the churches." The subtlety is that they had yielded to being satisfied with self-indulgence and self-satisfaction. With that posture, they had grown lukewarm to the Spiritual part of their soul and life, and began to modify and forget the Standards of God.

We must remind ourselves of where we are supposed to be in terms of The Eternal God. We are to have and maintain a relationship to God in Christ and know that positionally we, and The Church, are safe and secure in the hollow of our Lord's Hand – and – nothing – ever – shall be able to remove us from His Grip or separate us from His Love!

CONSIDER THESE THINGS WITH ME!

Flummoxed

It has become increasingly difficult to reach a determination regarding one's health diagnoses and treatments that are recommended. Just a brief scan of the various online news sources for March 19th, 2009 underscores the difficulty for one. For instance, NEWSMAX has the following panel under HEALTH: "(1) Lowering Cholesterol May Decrease Prostate Cancer Risk; (2) 'Smart Drug' Provigil May Be Addictive; (3) Frankincense Oil Kills Bladder Cancer Cells; (4) Being Obese Can Lead to Early Death; (5)Anti-Seizure Meds May Increase Heart Risks." The ABC News Page has this item: "Should Men Get Prostate Cancer Screening? Prostate Cancer Studies May Leave Men Flummoxed (confused; perplexed)....Dr. Eric Larson states: ...studies have not demonstrated that there is any benefit [to the prostate specific antigen screening] and there is certainly a good chance the PSA [prostate specific antigen] screening leads to procedures with complications and without benefit." USA Today has a post entitled: "Sorting Out Some Troubling Questions of PSA Screenings."

One of the above articles discusses a patient who followed a physician's recommendation to cease using Ibuprofen and switch to Naproxen. After he did so, he developed (1) an elevated PSA rating, and (2) pain when raising his right arm. The physician recommended further tests and going to a Urologist for further diagnosis. The patient decided on an alternative, namely, go back to the Ibuprofen and see if that will be beneficial. In his case, his PSA returned to normal and the pain was no longer present in his arm area. This is another instance where one can become Flummoxed (Confused; Perplexed). Lurking in the background are proponents of/for alternative medicines. In the midst of the ramblings, ruminations and discussion/debate in terms of the merits of using alternatives, one's confusion escalates. Shall one use Prescription Medications or choose an alternative? Will Niacin work as effectively as Pravachol; will Saw Palmetto be a good substitute for Flomax; will regular Coated Aspirin work as well as Plavix? Confusion reigns because people become torn between options – "Do I follow my instincts (or fears) – or – a Doctor in whom I have confidence? Do I need a second opinion? What will I do differently if I have a second opinion?"

The articles referenced above regarding Prostate Cancer all include: "A man will probably die of something else before he dies of Prostate Cancer!" The questions then become: "Do I wish to run the risk and become the 1 in a 1,000 who will die from Prostate Cancer? Or, should I run the risks of incontinence or basic castration by having the tests and ultimate surgery to remove the prostate? What is the possibility of the cancer metastasizing and spreading elsewhere in my body?" If a Urologist indicated one is in the lower 10% of possibly having prostate cancer, what decision should one make?

Almost 40 years ago, Dr. S.I. McMillen authored an intriguing book entitled: "None Of These Diseases." The back panel summary of this book asserts: "Medical professionals agree that there is a link between physical health and spiritual and emotional well-being. So it follows that the Bible's prescriptions for living that relate to temperance, the protection and nourishment of the body and mind, and sanitation will promote good health and vitality…God guaranteed a freedom from disease that modern medicine cannot duplicate. In None of These Diseases, he shows how medical science now supports the truths that have been in God's Word all along." The basis for his assertion are the words found in Exodus 15:26, "If you will diligently listen to the voice of the Lord your God, and do that which is right in his eyes, and give ear to his commandments and keep all his statutes, I will put none of the diseases on you that I put on the Egyptians, for I am the Lord, your healer." In this instance, the promise rested upon their obedience and compliance. By extension, the assertion refers to a more disciplined action regarding dietary instruction and preparation. Certain foods were to be avoided. Other foods had to be prepared as prescribed.

Questions: Is there a value to following the Dietary Codes of the Old Testament today? If they do not have a continuing value and benefit, why did God mandate them in the first place? What if we returned to a Biblical Approach in terms of dietary and sanitation requisites – might it prove that many of these diseases could be avoided? Suppose that our environmental and pollution concerns were more acute – could that make a significant difference in terms of health issues?

Some time ago, Jordan Rubin wrote a book that contained - The Maker's Diet - to influence people to follow the dietary laws set down by The Bible. He believes that following these laws…is the way that man was meant to eat. He believes…incorrect eating habits are to blame for many of the diseases and conditions that are so prevalent in industrialized society today…

Two Biblical Dietary Guidelines are emphasized:
Seafood - Leviticus 11:9-10

"These you may eat, of all that are in the waters. Everything in the waters that has fins and scales, whether in the seas or in the rivers, you may eat. But anything in the seas or the rivers that has not fins and scales, of the swarming creatures in the waters and of the living creatures that are in the waters, is detestable to you."

Simply, this means that fish with scales are intended to be eaten, such as salmon and trout, but smooth fish such as catfish and eels should not be eaten. It also means that crustaceans with hard shells such as lobster, crabs, and clams are not to be eaten.

Other Meats – Leviticus 11:3, 7-8

"Whatever parts the hoof and is cloven-footed and chews the cud, among the animals, you may eat."

"And the pig, because it parts the hoof and is cloven-footed but does not chew the cud, is unclean to you. You shall not eat any of their flesh, and you shall not touch their carcasses; they are unclean to you."

Simply – ham, sausage, bacon, ribs, pork chops, loins, etc. should be avoided.

Rather than being flummoxed with Prescription or over-the-counter medications, perhaps we could and should try a Biblical approach and endeavor to be focused on what God recommended and be healthier as a result.

This concept reminds one of Daniel 1:8-17... The issue was whether or not they would be compromised and forced to eat meats offered to idols. Daniel and his friends were principled and committed to the Lord. They refused!

"Daniel resolved that he would not defile himself with the king's food, or with the wine that he drank. Therefore he asked the chief of the eunuchs to allow him not to defile himself. And God gave Daniel favor and compassion in the sight of the chief of the eunuchs, and the chief of the eunuchs said to Daniel, I fear my lord the king, who assigned your food and your drink; for why should he see that you were in worse condition than the youths who are of your own age? So you would endanger my head with the king. Then Daniel said to the steward whom the chief of the eunuchs had assigned over Daniel, Hananiah, Mishael, and Azariah, Test your servants for ten days; let us be given vegetables to eat and water to drink. Then let our appearance and the appearance of the youths who eat the king's food be observed by you, and deal with your servants according to what you see. So he listened to them in this matter, and tested them for ten days. At the end of ten days it was seen that they were better in appearance and fatter in flesh than all the youths who ate the king's food. So the steward took away their food and the wine they were to drink, and gave them vegetables. As for these four youths, God gave them learning and skill in all literature and wisdom, and Daniel had understanding in all visions and dreams."

We know that the Lord honored Daniel and his friends for their commitment to Him and their steadfastness in terms of the cultural war and pressures that were before them. Did it always go well for them in the culture of Babylon? No! We remember that Daniel was thrown into a Lion's Den – but God delivered him unscathed. We know that Shadrach, Meshach and Abednego were thrown into a fiery furnace – but were delivered unharmed. Why? In the words of a southern gospel song - because – they wouldn't bow, they wouldn't bend – and as a result – they didn't burn.

One slight wrinkle for us is the moment of Peter's Vision in Acts 10:9-16. we read: "About noon the following day as they were on their journey and approaching the city, Peter went up on the roof to pray. He became hungry and wanted something to eat, and while the meal was being prepared, he fell into a trance. He saw heaven opened and something like a large sheet being let down to earth by its four corners. It contained all kinds of four-footed animals, as well as reptiles of the earth and birds of the air. Then a voice told him, Get up, Peter. Kill and eat. Surely not, Lord! Peter replied. I have never eaten anything impure or unclean. The voice spoke to him a second time, Do not call anything impure that God has made clean. This happened three times, and immediately the sheet was taken back to heaven." A new day and a new approach – new rules! Why? In part, because Peter had to go to the Gentiles with the Gospel. He was reluctant but it was God's expanding work He wanted done.

It would do us well to remember the words of I Samuel 2:30, "Therefore the Lord, the God of Israel, declares: I promised that your house and the house of your father should go in and out before me forever…for those who honor me I will honor, and those who despise me shall be lightly esteemed."

CONSIDER THESE THINGS WITH ME!

Revolting Development

Many years ago, a comedy radio program entitled: "The Life of Riley", featured a very typical and ordinary hard-working character who was trying to survive and to make ends meet. When he was confronted by tenuous, frustrating or exasperating situations, his expression was always: "What A Revolting Development This Is!" One is caused to wonder how often Riley would be expressing – "what a revolting development this is!" – if he was a true character who was alive today. The Novelist, Ernest Hemingway is quoted as having mused: "You know that fiction, prose rather, is possibly the roughest trade of all in writing. You do not have the reference, the old important reference. You have the sheet of blank paper, the pencil, and the obligation to invent truer than things can be true. You have to take what is not palpable and make it completely palpable and also have it seem normal and so that it can become a part of experience of the person who reads it." Another person observed: "Truth may be stranger than fiction, but fiction is truer."

President Obama appeared on The Tonight Show on March 19, 2009. In the midst of his various comments he said in terms of "reinvestment" that "the rich can afford to pay more taxes…" I can almost hear Riley utter: "what a revolting development this is"! This entire concept of "reinvestment" is Washington-Speak for New Taxation that will essentially tax the wealthier Americans so additional Welfare and Benefits can be given to the poor, non-working, or under-achievers. This causes one to wonder where all of this "take from one to give to another" will end. It can be called many things – Welfare State, Socialism, Taxation Without Adequate Representation, etc. – but the bottom-line is that it is wrong, wrong, wrong from start to finish. People should be motivated to be productive! This system generates the spirit of entitlement! It is quite simply – "gimme, gimme, gimme" and "more, more, more!"

Some people have referenced this as a type of Robin Hood approach. More than 70 years ago, The Adventures of Robin Hood was popularized in film. The story is intriguing: "When Richard the Lionhearted, the King of England, is taken captive by Leopold of Austria while returning from the Crusades, his brother John takes power and proceeds to oppress the Saxon commoners. Prince John raises their taxes, supposedly to raise Richard's ransom, but in reality to secure his own position on the throne. One man stands in his way, the Saxon Robin, Earl of Locksley. Robin goes alone to see Prince John and announces to John's assembled supporters and a contemptuous Maid Marian that he will do all in his power to oppose John and restore Richard to his rightful place. He then escapes, in spite of the efforts of John's men. His lands and title now forfeited, Robin takes refuge in Sherwood Forest. One day, Robin and his men capture a large party of Normans transporting the collected taxes through Sherwood. King Richard returns to England disguised as a monk. Richard and his escort travel to Sherwood Forest to find Robin. Richard is soon restored to the throne; he exiles his brother, pardons the outlaws, returns Robin's title and possessions.

The essential difference between the fictional Robin Hood and the actions of our day is that Robin Hood was a defender of justice and what was right. He championed decency and order, and his activities underscored that point. The problem we have today, although complex, could begin with the Work Ethic. A "welfare State" will be a very weak one. We will (a) run out of assets and resources, and (b) we will lose the ability and motivation to defend ourselves. This will weaken the nation and cause it to become an easy prey for possible enemies. The "Spend and Tax Us" philosophy of government is very shortsighted and will soon produce a cash shortfall and insolvency.

The Biblical focus is clear and unambiguous.

II Thessalonians 3:10-12, "when we were with you, we gave you this command: If anyone is not willing to work, let him not eat.

For we hear that some among you walk in idleness, not busy at work, but busybodies. Now such persons we command and encourage in the Lord Jesus Christ to do their work quietly and to earn their own living." The basic thrust is that God made man to be industrious and to be a provider – not to be lazy and a moocher.

I Timothy 5:7-8, "Command these things as well, so that they may be without reproach. But if anyone does not provide for his relatives, and especially for members of his household, he has denied the faith and is worse than an unbeliever." The basic thrust is personal responsibility and active in meeting the necessities of life for one's own household and extended family.

There was an interesting moment of Obfuscation recently. It is defined by The American Heritage Dictionary as: "To make so confused or opaque as to be difficult to perceive or understand…To render indistinct or dim; darken…" In a caustic sense, it is tempting to allow that as a better description of the Houses of Congress, the more fitting title should be The Houses of Obfuscation. Few of our circumlocutious politicians can give a simple cogent response to a direct question. They all have their "spin" and/or "talking-points" so well defined that they just parrot out their responses regardless of the question posed. It comes across as programmed, Washington-Speak, unclear diatribe. It has become all too easy to both ignore and turn off those who comment in such a manner.

During the program, 60 Minutes, there was a rare and poignant moment. Steve Kroft was interviewing President Obama regarding the economy, recession factors, etc. The President responded to a couple of the inquiries with laughter. POLITICO reports the moment in this way: "President Barack Obama said he believes the global financial system remains at risk of implosion with the failure of Citigroup or AIG, which could touch off "an even more destructive recession and potentially depression. His remarks came in a 60 Minutes interview in which he was pressed by Steve Kroft for laughing and chuckling several times while discussing the perilous state of the world's economy. You're sitting here. And you're— you are laughing. You are laughing about some of these problems. Are people going to look at this and say, 'I mean, he's sitting there just making jokes about money—' How do you deal with— I mean: explain…." The article goes on to state: "…Are you punch-drunk? Kroft said. 'No, no. There's gotta be a little gallows humor to get you through the day,' Obama said, with a laugh…"

"One wonders if its construed as "gallows humor" by those whose employment is ended; savings accounts shrinking; investments lost; foreclosure possibility; recession obvious; fear of depression looming – where is the humor – gallows or otherwise – Mr. President. When our nation is stampeding toward bankruptcy and an uncertain future for the next generation – where is the humor, Mr. President? What is the punch line? Why is it so few are laughing? If its funny, why are so many anguished? Please! Explain the punch-line for us! One commentator mused: I guess I'll have to retire on 40% of what I thought I had! Is that the joke, Mr. President? In case you haven't noticed, no one is laughing!"

It would be good if our nation and leaders could remember how good God has been to this nation and the abundance of His Blessings upon us. To forget this goodness and blessing is to relegate oneself into the realm of the foolish. Basically, a fool is one who "despises wisdom and walks in folly." "The word for 'fool' is used in Scripture with respect to moral more than to intellectual deficiencies - The 'fool' is not so much lacking in mental powers, as one who misuses them. In Scripture the 'fool'...is the person who casts off the fear of God, and thinks and acts as if he could safely disregard the eternal principles of God's righteousness. Essentially, a fool thus chooses to disregard God and His wisdom (Unger's Bible Dictionary)." Proverbs 12:15 states: "The way of a fool is right in his own eyes, But he who heeds counsel is wise." And Proverbs 28:26 adds, "He who trusts in his own heart is a fool, "But whoever walks wisely will be delivered." It would be good to take note of a Proverbs 26:1-12. This section of Scripture addresses the subject of a "fool" and concludes with this declaration: "Do you see a man who is wise in his own eyes? There is more hope for a fool than for him." We don't need to travel this road as individuals or as a nation. We still have opportunity to return to the Lord Who stands ready to show us His mercy and His pardon. The fool will say: "There is no God! (Psalm 14:1)" The wise will Come To Jesus. There's still room at the Cross for you!

    We should not expect God to bless America – or us as an individual - when we so willfully ignore Him and His Word. We can only reply to the actions of our nation, elected representatives, and non-productive citizens in the words from The Life of Riley: "What a revolting development this is!"

CONSIDER THESE THINGS WITH ME!

Concluding Thoughts

As one journeys through life, the words written by the Apostle Paul in I Corinthians 13:12 become more apparent – "Now we see but a poor reflection as in a mirror; then we shall see face to face. Now I know in part; then I shall know fully, even as I am fully known." The New Living Translations states it: "Now we see things imperfectly as in a poor mirror, but then we will see everything with perfect clarity. All that I know now is partial and incomplete, but then I will know everything completely, just as God knows me now."

My hope is that the Essays, although not connected by an overall theme, will nevertheless resonate because of the Biblical principles that serve as Guideposts for the traveler through life. Perhaps it will stir ones heart, mind and soul to be both inquisitive and practical in ones approach to life and living. It would be similar to the words attributed to George Bernard Shaw: "Some men see things as they are and say why - I dream things that never were and say why not."

As these concluding thoughts are being written, my thoughts and prayers are with a Granddaughter and her husband as they begin their journey to Eastern Europe to adopt their three and one-half year old son and return with him to the United States. The practical application of Scripture that was shared with them are these words:

"We'll be praying that you have a safe and satisfactory journey... We are also praying there will be no hitch in any detail... We somewhat sense your anticipation... We're eager to see and hold and know and enjoy Great One #4...

Be safe! Be assured from the word in Jeremiah 29:11 (NLT) - "For I know the plans I have for you, says the LORD. They are plans for good and not for disaster, to give you a future and a hope." And then - from The Message: "I know what I'm doing. I have it all planned out - plans to take care of you, not abandon you, plans to give you the future you hope for..."

These same words are true for each of us as we face all of what is known and the unknowns in and for our lives. Words contained in a Worship Chorus that have become a reminder of God's Faithfulness are:

God Will Make A Way

By a roadway in the wilderness, He'll lead me
And rivers in the desert will I see
Heaven and earth will fade
But His Word will still remain
He will do something new today.

God will make a way, Where there seems to be no way.
He works in ways we cannot see, He will make a way for me.
He will be my guide, Hold me closely to His side.
With love and strength for each new day,
He will make a way, He will make a way.

My hope for you is in the words of Ephesians 6:10-13 (NLT)

"A final word: Be strong with the Lord's mighty power. Put on all of God's armor so that you will be able to stand firm against all strategies and tricks of the Devil. For we are not fighting against people made of flesh and blood, but against the evil rulers and authorities of the unseen world, against those mighty powers of darkness who rule this world, and against wicked spirits in the heavenly realms. Use every piece of God's armor to resist the enemy in the time of evil, so that after the battle you will still be standing firm."

About the Author

Pastor James Perry was born and reared in Brooklyn, NY and lived there for the first twenty years of his life. In the providence of God, he went to work at Lakeside Bible Conference in Carmel, NY and roomed in a two-man cabin with one who was the President of the Student Body of Columbia Bible College in Columbia, SC. His room mate was persistent throughout the summer as he asked James whether or not he knew God's purpose and will for his life. At the end of the summer, James Perry rode to Columbia, SC with some friends who had enrolled in Columbia Bible College, his thought being that he would hitchhike back home.

The Lord had other plans for his life. He was allowed to enroll and begin studying for the ministry there from 1954-57. He completed his College work at Covenant College, now located at Lookout Mountain, GA and went on to Covenant Theological Seminary in St. Louis, MO. He completed that training in 1964.

Part of the Lord's plan for his life was to bring a beautiful Christian young woman into his life during his freshman year. They were united in marriage in 1956 and have been partners in ministry from that point of time onward. The Lord has given them four children, fourteen grandchildren, and four great-grandchildren.

James Perry has served as a Pastor for more than forty-six years in churches from New Jersey to Colorado to Alabama - with some in-between. He found great joy in doing so.

Pastor Perry said, "this is my first effort in publishing a tome and if it has a reasonable positive response I may try to compile another. Thank you for taking the time to read these chapters."

www.ingramcontent.com/pod-product-compliance
Lightning Source LLC
Chambersburg PA
CBHW061646040426
42446CB00010B/1602